word alive

n-depth Small Group Bible Studies

STUDY GUIDE

Philippians

MW01174059

PHILIPPIANS

Paul's thank-you letter

Edwin Walhout

FAITH ALIVE®
Christian Resources

Grand Rapids, Michigan

Unless otherwise noted, Scripture quotations in this publication are from the
HOLY BIBLE, NEW INTERNATIONAL VERSION, © 1973, 1978, 1984,
International Bible Society. Used by permission of Zondervan Bible Publishers.

Cover photo: The Image Bank

Faith Alive Christian Resources published by CRC Publications.
Word Alive: In-depth Small Group Bible Studies
Philippians: Paul's Thank-You Letter (Study Guide), © 2002 by CRC Publications,
2850 Kalamazoo Ave. SE, Grand Rapids, MI 49560. All rights reserved. With the
exception of brief excerpts for review purposes, no part of this book may be
reproduced in any manner whatsoever without written permission from the
publisher. Printed in the United States of America on recycled paper. ⊕

We welcome your comments. Call us at 1-800-333-8300 or e-mail us at
editors@faithaliveresources.org.

ISBN 1-56212-846-9

10 9 8 7 6 5 4 3 2 1

Contents

Introduction

Picture yourself in prison. You've been moved from one jail to another, and now you're chained to a guard all day, every day. For more than two years you've been waiting to appeal your case, and you don't know how much longer you'll have to wait. On top of all this, you're here on false charges. You haven't broken the law, but you're at the mercy of the legal system to deal with you as it sees fit.

What will you do with your time here? What *can* you do? At least you're allowed visitors, so you can talk with people who come to look after your needs. You can also talk with the guard you're chained to. And there are lots of people you'd like to write to in the places where you used to work, so you could spend some time writing letters, especially to thank your dear friends who've sent help along the way.

As you do this, you know that the best thing you can do is to keep your mind focused on glorifying God and to tell everyone around you that the greatest thing in life is Jesus Christ.

That's what the apostle Paul did. While in prison, he wrote a thank-you letter to his Christian friends in the Roman colony of Philippi. And he took the opportunity to encourage them with all kinds of practical advice for their own struggles, urging them to keep serving the Lord Jesus with all their strength, to the glory of God.

Paul's example of putting God first in his life, after the example of Christ himself, is truly remarkable and inspiring. As you learn more about Paul's situation and the joy-filled, wise counsel he sends to the Philippians, may "the grace of the Lord Jesus Christ be with your spirit" (Phil. 4:23). Walk with the Lord each day, press on toward the goal of full life in Christ, and rejoice in the God of your salvation!

—Paul Faber, for Faith Alive Christian Resources

Edwin Walhout, author of this study guide and the accompanying leader's guide, is a retired minister of the Christian Reformed Church living in Grand Rapids, Michigan. He has taught in Christian schools in Michigan and New Jersey; served as a pastor of churches in Minnesota, New York, and Massachusetts; and worked as an editor of adult education materials for CRC Publications.

Why did Paul write this letter?

1

PHILIPPIANS 1:1-2

Paul in Chains

In a Nutshell

This opening lesson of our study introduces us to Paul's letter to the Philippians by tracing events that led to Paul's becoming a prisoner in Rome. We can piece together most of the story from Acts 21-28. This background is important for helping us understand many of the things Paul discusses in his letter. We also examine the address and greeting of this letter—what a wealth of information they contain!

Philippians 1:1-2

¹Paul and Timothy, servants of Christ Jesus,

To all the saints in Christ Jesus at Philippi, together with the overseers and deacons:

²Grace and peace to you from God our Father and the Lord Jesus Christ.

Additional reading: Acts 13-28

How Paul Became a Prisoner in Rome

Philippians is one of Paul's four *prison letters*. The others are Colossians, Ephesians, and Philemon. These writings are called *prison letters* because Paul wrote them while he was a prisoner in Rome. "I am in chains," he writes (Phil. 1:13; see Eph. 6:20; Col. 4:3, 18; Philem. 13). These letters come at a relatively late period in Paul's life, around A.D. 60-63. In fact, Paul refers to himself in one of them as "an old man" (Philem. 9). The story of how Paul came to be a prisoner in Rome is told in Acts 21-28, and some additional background is available in Acts 13-20. Here's a brief summary of Paul's long ordeal:

Near the end of his third missionary journey, most of it spent directing outreach from Ephesus, Paul made a quick trip to Greece by way of Philippi, Thessalonica, Berea, and Corinth.

Then he retraced his steps, bypassing Ephesus on his way to Jerusalem.

Why was Paul on his way to Jerusalem? Paul and his companions were bringing a gift of money to the Christians there. For quite some time, Paul had been collecting this money, with Titus as his representative (2 Cor. 8:1-6), to help Christians in Jerusalem who'd been struck by poverty. In recent years there'd been a huge famine in the Roman world, and it had hit hard in Judea (see Acts 11:27-30).

The closer Paul got to Jerusalem, however, the more warnings he received that he would face hardships there (20:22-23, 38; 21:4, 10-12). Why? He was going for a good purpose, so why not continue? The trouble was that many people in Jerusalem did not trust Paul. The Jewish authorities there despised him because he had changed from being a Jewish Pharisee to a Christian missionary. And the Christian Jews there had heard rumors that Paul was telling converts they didn't have to obey God's law anymore. Actually, Paul was saying it wasn't important to keep all of the Jewish rituals anymore—such as circumcision, avoiding all "unclean" foods, and so on. And this teaching was right in line with what the Jerusalem Christians had decided in a special council about five years earlier (Acts 15). So when he arrived in Jerusalem, Paul was careful to show that he was living in obedience to the law. He even joined with several others in purification rites connected with a vow they had made (18:18; 21:20-25).

Still, trouble broke out when some Jews thought Paul had brought some Gentiles with him into the temple there—where Jewish law stated that Gentiles were not allowed. This false assumption, along with the rumors that had been circulating, stirred the people into an angry mob. Paul soon found himself in the midst of a riot in which he would have been killed if Roman soldiers hadn't come to restore order and arrest him (21:27-34). But even after Paul was put in prison for his own safety, his enemies plotted to kill him (23:10, 12-15). So the Roman authorities took Paul to their regional headquarters in Caesarea, about 50 miles (80 km) away.

In Caesarea Paul waited in prison for more than two years for the regional governors, first Felix and then Festus, to decide what to do with him (24:27). Finally Paul appealed to be tried by Caesar in Rome (25:10-12). He was entitled to do this because he was a Roman citizen (16:37-39; 22:25-29). So off he went to Rome, where he waited as a prisoner for another two years to appeal his case to Caesar (26:32-27:2)—and that's where we find Paul as he writes to his Christian friends in Philippi.

Why Paul Wrote This Letter

While waiting for Caesar to decide his case, "Paul stayed there in his own rented house and welcomed all who came to see him," preaching the gospel "boldly and without hindrance" (Acts 28:30). At least he wasn't locked up in a cold, dark dungeon. But as a prisoner living under house arrest "with a soldier to guard him" (28:16), Paul did have expenses to pay for his upkeep.

When the Christians in Philippi heard about this, they took up a generous collection and sent a man named Epaphroditus from their church to bring their gifts to Paul in Rome (Phil. 2:25; 4:18). So Paul's initial purpose in writing this letter was to thank them for their support. As he wrote, Paul took the opportunity also to encourage the Philippians about living the Christian life.

A secondary reason for writing, of course, was simply that Paul had the rare opportunity to do so. (There was no convenient postal or courier service in those days.) Since Epaphroditus would return to Philippi, Paul took advantage of the occasion to write a thank-you letter and to send it along with this man who had become a trusted friend (2:25-30).

How Paul Addresses His Letter

The letter that Epaphroditus carried to the church in Philippi would have been written on a scroll, probably a rolled-up sheet of papyrus. A letter in those days usually began by identifying the writer. Next it would identify the recipient. So this is how Paul addressed his letter:

> Paul and Timothy, servants of Christ Jesus,
>
> To all the saints in Christ Jesus at Philippi, together with the overseers and deacons: . . . (Phil. 1:1)

Many of Paul's letters in the New Testament begin with a similar kind of address. Because there may have been other men by the name of Paul who wrote letters, it probably was essential to include a description that identified Paul as an apostle of Christ or at least as a servant of Christ, depending on who his intended readers were. In 2 Corinthians, for example, we find Paul identifying himself as "an apostle of Christ Jesus by the will of God" (2 Cor. 1:1), and we learn later that Paul wrote that letter, at least in part, to defend himself and the gospel message against false teachings being circulated in

Corinth by other teachers, who were calling themselves "super-apostles" (11:5).

Apparently the church in Philippi had not encountered as much trouble or distraction with false teachers as the church in Corinth had. In fact, Paul's letter to the Philippians rings with thanks and joy for the believers' faithful "partnership in the gospel" (Phil. 1:5). So in this letter Paul's identification can understandably be more general as he states, in effect, *I am the Paul who is a servant [slave, Greek] of Christ Jesus.*

Timothy, who is with Paul in Rome, greets the readers also. (Timothy's name also appears in the greetings of several other letters of Paul: 2 Corinthians, Colossians, 1 and 2 Thessalonians, and Philemon.) It may be that Timothy is mentioned because he is actually transcribing the letter as Paul dictates it. Paul may well have poor eyesight by this time in his life—or perhaps ever since his blinding encounter with Jesus outside Damascus (Acts 9:3-9, 18; 22:6-13; 26:13)—so he may be employing someone else to inscribe his letter.

We also know that Paul often used the dictation method in other letters. For example, in 2 Thessalonians 3:17 we find this personal note: "I, Paul, write this greeting in my own hand, which is the distinguishing mark in all my letters. This is how I write" (see also 1 Cor. 16:21; Gal. 6:11; Col. 4:18). In light of these examples, it seems safe to say that after using the help of a scribe (probably Timothy) to write down most of his letter to the Philippians, Paul may well have written the closing remarks with his own hand (see Phil. 4:21-23).

Notice how Paul formulates the next part of the address: "To all the saints in Christ Jesus at Philippi . . ." (Phil. 1:1). If we wonder what Paul means here by "saints," it's important to know that he's talking about all the Christians in the church at Philippi. The word *saint* is related to the word *sanctification,* which refers to being made holy, or set apart for service to God (though not in separation from the world). Everyone who is sanctified by believing in Jesus as Lord and Savior and who lives by the power of the Spirit of Christ is a saint. Everyone who is a Christian, then, is a saint. So Paul is addressing all the Christians in Philippi.

To emphasize his point that this letter is for "all the saints," Paul notes that he is grouping them "together with the overseers and deacons" (1:1). Though churches in those days were not highly organized, they did have elders and deacons who had special functions to help the congregation work together for Jesus' sake. With this in mind, it's probably best for us not to make too much of the word "overseers," which comes from a Greek word often translated as "bishops" (see KJV, RSV, NRSV). The Philippian church leaders in Paul's day certainly did not have the authority we associate with bishops in some churches today. As John Calvin suggests in his *Commentary on Philippians,* Paul likely has in mind here the elders of the church. Further, Paul does not emphasize a great distinction between clergy and laity (or laypeople), as some churches do (for example, giving preferential treatment to clergy, saying that only the clergy may read God's Word and must interpret it for the laity, and so on). Paul's address in Philippians shows clearly that this letter is meant for all members equally.

A Wonderful Greeting

Proceeding with a benediction ("good word") for all, Paul says, "Grace and peace to you from God our Father and the Lord Jesus Christ." This wonderful greeting occurs almost word for word in every one of Paul's letters in the New Testament. And although it's a standardized greeting for Paul, it's a meaningful one. Think of the depths of meaning behind the words "grace" and "peace" in connection with "God our Father and the Lord Jesus Christ." Long chapters and big books have been written in attempts to explain the depths and interconnections of these words and phrases.

In simple terms we can say that "grace" refers to God's gift of love to us in Christ ("by grace you have been saved"—Eph. 2:5, 8) and that "peace" refers to the wonderful blessedness of living in line with God (going back to the Old Testament virtue of *shalom*). The two together remind us that the gospel of grace in the New Testament is built on the promises of peace and blessing in the Old Testament—and much more. More specifically, grace is the blessing God provides us through Jesus so that we can overcome the power of sin in our lives through the ongoing work of the Holy Spirit. And peace is the result of that grace. Peace is the blessing of a well-ordered, harmonious life—not only for us as individuals but also for society as a whole.

Additional Notes

1:1—"Paul and Timothy." Most scholars believe this letter was written around A.D. 61 in Rome, but pinpointing the events of Paul's life can be difficult. It's possible that Paul was about ten to twelve years younger than Jesus, since Paul was apparently a student in Jerusalem under Gamaliel around the time of Christ's death and the outpouring of the Holy Spirit (see Acts 5:34; 7:58; 22:3). But since we don't know exactly when Jesus or Paul or Timothy was born, we can only guess how old Paul was when he went to Rome as a prisoner. Perhaps he was about 50 years old, and at that time Timothy may have been about 30.

"servants of Christ Jesus." The Greek word *douloi* is often translated as "servants," but it really means "slaves." Far from inhibiting or crushing a person's spirit, becoming a slave to Jesus liberates, expands, and fulfills. Paul and Timothy are willing and grateful slaves of their Master and Savior, the Lord Jesus. In our times the concept of Christian slavery is not popular, but it ought to characterize each of us. "You have been set free from sin and have become slaves to righteousness," writes Paul in Romans 6:18. And the righteousness we claim is not our own, but Christ's—what a gift!

"Philippi." Paul's missionary strategy was usually to visit large, important cities in a given region, establishing churches that could then radiate the gospel message to surrounding areas. Philippi was just such a city. Named after Philip of Macedon, the father of Alexander the Great, this prosperous city became a Roman colony where many ex-soldiers of the Roman army came to settle down. Citizens of this city had the same legal rights as if the city were in Italy itself. See Acts 16 for the account of how the church was established there.

1:2—"peace." Our English word *peace* translates the Greek word *eirene,* which in turn translates the Hebrew word *shalom.* This is what the Jews expected the Messiah to bring, a condition in which the Jewish nation would be independent and supreme, enjoying a golden age of Jewish prosperity. When Jesus refused to be pressed into that mold, the people rejected him as an impostor. But the *shalom* Jesus truly brings is not first of all political, dependent on military might or economic success. True *shalom* is spiritual and moral, bringing "the peace of God, which transcends all understanding" (Phil. 4:7). *Shalom* is characterized by the blessed life lived in faithfulness to Jesus as Savior and Lord.

GENERAL DISCUSSION

1. What was the wisdom in Paul's going to Jerusalem, especially since he knew he would have a rough reception there? (See Acts 20:22; 21:4, 10-36.)

2. Explain why so many people in Jerusalem distrusted Paul, some of them even hating him.

3. What makes a person a saint?

4. Reflect on *grace* and *peace*. What do these words mean, and how are their meanings interrelated?

SMALL GROUP SESSION IDEAS

Note: The following session plan is divided into several timed sections to help you keep pace for your meeting time. The suggested times add up to 60-75 minutes for a full session. Use whatever time your group needs or is most comfortable with. Also feel free to choose or adapt these ideas to suit your needs.

Opening (10-15 minutes)

Pray/Worship—As you begin this first session of your study of Philippians, pray for a gracious and peaceful Christian spirit among you. Be open to the truth of God's Word and the power of God's Spirit as you discuss Scripture together.

If you'd like to sing together, you could do so at this time with a song that focuses on God's grace and peace in Christ Jesus, such as "My God, How Wonderful You Are" or "I Know Not Why God's Wondrous Grace."

Share—This sharing time is intended to help everyone start focusing on the study material for the session. This can also be a time for introductions if any of you haven't met each other or studied together before. (If you have prayer concerns you'd like to share, it may be best to do so nearer the end of the session, while preparing for closing prayer—see the Closing section below.) As your study of Philippians unfolds, you may find that it's helpful at this point also to review themes from previous lessons or to talk about goals you've set and group projects you've decided to do.

Focus—For this introductory lesson on the background and opening of Philippians, try to keep the following focus questions in mind: *Why did Paul write this letter? What circumstances was Paul in as he wrote, and why? What does all this have to do with me? With my group? With my church?*

Growing (35-40 minutes)
Read—You may like to read together the Scripture for your lesson and to review portions of the study guide notes before moving into your discussion time. Since our Scripture for this lesson is only two verses long, perhaps just one person could read it aloud for everyone else to hear. If you also want to read something from the book of Acts about Paul and the background of this letter, you could take turns reading verses or paragraphs from Acts 21:27-36 (telling briefly how Paul got into trouble in Jerusalem), Acts 25:8-12 (telling why Paul went to Rome), and Acts 28:16, 30-31 (describing Paul's situation in Rome).

Discuss—The questions listed in the General Discussion section are mostly informational and objective (especially in this first lesson of our study) and will sometimes encourage personal reflection that can help everyone work out a practical response to the lesson material. Additional questions that encourage personal reflection and sharing are included below.

• How would you react if a visiting preacher came into your church and began criticizing traditions you hold to? Are there some traditions you could do without? Some you couldn't do without? Explain.

• What have you learned about the apostle Paul in this lesson? Can you picture yourself living the kind of life he had? Share your thoughts and impressions about Paul with the rest of the group.

• What have you learned about *grace* and *peace* in this lesson? In what ways can (or will) this affect your relationship with God? Your relationships with others?

Goalsetting (5 minutes)
As you near the close of your session, try to determine one or more concrete things you can do as a result of this lesson.

- One useful goal you might set for the coming week may be to think of yourself in Paul's place as his enemies in Jerusalem attack and plot against him, or as he languishes in prison for years, dealing with many difficulties. Reflect on your own relationship with God. In what ways should it be more like Paul's? In what ways are you reflecting the "attitude . . . of Christ" already (Phil. 2:5)? Praise God and ask for continued guidance in your daily living.

- Another goal might be to look ahead in Philippians to see what's coming next. Along with committing yourself to prepare for the next lesson, you might also want to read through the entire letter, since it's only four chapters long. Then perhaps you could pick out a passage and reflect on it awhile, asking God to help you understand and live by it.

- You could also look ahead in this study to see if there's a follow-up project you could do with some or all of your group. Step out of your comfort zones, if necessary. Pray about the ideas presented as Group Projects at the end of some of the lessons in this booklet. Ask for guidance and an open heart to be available for service in Jesus' name. You may be surprised by the way God responds!

Closing (10-15 minutes)
Preparing for Prayer—All of you are welcome to mention personal concerns and praise items that you'd like to bring to God in prayer. Try also to focus on matters that have come up in connection with the lesson material, such as new insights you've gained, or goals you'd like to set. As a group, try to maintain a genuine pastoral atmosphere, in which you listen to and care for each other and are ready to help and to build each other up.

Prayer—As you close in prayer, thank God for the time you've had together, follow up on prayer requests that have been mentioned, and ask for the Lord's guidance as you continue this study of Philippians. May the "grace and peace" of God in Christ go with you as you part till your next meeting.

How Paul's trouble affected two churches.

2

Two Churches: Philippi and Rome

In a Nutshell

How did Christian people react when they heard Paul was in serious trouble? As we noted in lesson 1, Paul was now a prisoner in Rome, waiting for a hearing with Caesar. The church in Philippi responded by sending Paul encouragement and financial support. The reaction in Rome, however, was mixed. Some of the Christians there were sympathetic to Paul and became stronger in faith because of Paul's example. Others thought he had done wrong—at least in his teaching about the law—and that he deserved the trouble he was in.

Philippians 1:3-18

3I thank my God every time I remember you. 4In all my prayers for all of you, I always pray with joy 5because of your partnership in the gospel from the first day until now, 6being confident of this, that he who began a good work in you will carry it on to completion until the day of Christ Jesus.

7It is right for me to feel this way about all of you, since I have you in my heart; for whether I am in chains or defending and confirming the gospel, all of you share in God's grace with me. 8God can testify how I long for all of you with the affection of Christ Jesus.

9And this is my prayer: that your love may abound more and more in knowledge and depth of insight, 10so that you may be able to discern what is best and may be pure and blameless until the day of Christ, 11filled with the fruit of righteousness that comes through Jesus Christ—to the glory and praise of God.

12Now I want you to know, brothers, that what has happened to me has really served to advance the gospel. 13As a result, it has become clear throughout the whole palace guard and to everyone else that I am in chains for Christ. 14Because of my chains, most of the brothers in the Lord have been encouraged to speak the word of God more courageously and fearlessly. 15It is true that some preach Christ out of envy and rivalry, but others out of goodwill. 16The latter do so in love, knowing that I am put here for the defense of the gospel. 17The former preach Christ out of selfish ambition, not sincerely, supposing that they can stir up trouble for me while I am in chains. 18But what does it matter?

The important thing is that in every way, is preached. And because of this I rejoice. whether from false motives or true, Christ

The Church in Philippi

It's interesting to see that the first thing Paul does in the body of his letter is to give praise for all of the people in the Philippian church. "I thank my God every time I remember you," he writes. "In all my prayers for all of you, I always pray with joy because of your partnership in the gospel from the first day until now, being confident of this, that he who began a good work in you will carry it on to completion until the day of Christ Jesus" (Phil. 1:3- 6). Think of some of the other letters Paul wrote—such as Galatians. That letter is full of warning and chastising. Compare the letters from Jesus to the seven churches in the book of Revelation: they usually begin with praise, if there is any to be mentioned, and then go on to criticism, if any is needed (see Rev. 2-3).

Paul is thankful and perhaps even proud of the church in Philippi (in a righteous sort of way), and he states, "It is right for me to feel this way about all of you" (Phil. 1:7). It's not that Paul takes any credit for starting their church some years ago, but rather, as he puts it, because "all of you share in God's grace with me" (1:7). Paul knows that it's only by God's grace that he himself has been saved, and he sees the same grace at work in the Philippian church. So he remains deeply interested in the Philippians' continued faith and service. He adds, "God can testify how I long for all of you with the affection of Christ Jesus" (1:8). This is the way we all ought to feel about all other Christians and all other churches.

Because Paul is thankful and deeply concerned for the Philippians' continued welfare in the faith, he can pray for their progress to continue—namely, "that [their] love may abound more and more" (1:9). And what will be the evidence of their growth in love? "Knowledge and depth of insight" (1:9). But knowledge of what, and insight into what? Into "what is best," says Paul. And "what is best"—that is, what aligns with God's good will for people in terms of *shalom*—will be proven in the results of being "pure and blameless" and being "filled with the fruit of righteousness" (1:10-11).

In Luke 6:43-44 Jesus says, "No good tree bears bad fruit, nor does a bad tree bear good fruit. Each tree is recognized by its own fruit." Paul is saying the same thing here.

What difference does becoming a Christian make in the way you live your life? The difference is that by the power of the

Spirit of Christ you now bear the fruit of righteousness in your life. In other words, you live a righteous life. That's what Paul prays for concerning the body of Christ in Philippi, and we all ought to pray the same thing for all Christians (including ourselves)—that we may show our faith in the way we live.

We must be careful, however, not to concentrate on ourselves or on our own circle of believers. If that happens, the pursuit of a righteous life can lead to being self-righteous—proud of our own humility, for example! Instead, as Paul explains, we need to do all this "to the glory and praise of God" (Phil. 1:11). God is the one who gives us life. God is the one who has given us grace through Jesus. God is also the one who sends the Holy Spirit to sanctify us, making us saints. As Paul himself knew so well, we need to live in such a way that we give all praise and glory to our Maker, Redeemer, and Sanctifier.

How Paul Is Doing as a Prisoner

Paul next gives the Philippians a description of what is happening to him. He is a prisoner of the Roman empire, but he is also an official citizen of that empire. So he has certain rights that noncitizens do not have. Paul is entitled to a fair trial by Caesar himself. And he is kept in minimum-security lockup while waiting for his trial, under what we would call house arrest—chained to a soldier of the palace guard to keep him from escaping.

Paul explains to the church in Philippi that "what has happened to [him] has really served to advance the gospel" (1:12). How so? Well, think about what it must have been like for the Roman soldiers who had to be chained to this prisoner for hours at a time. If you were one of those soldiers, you'd have to listen to whatever the prisoner might decide to talk about—even if you weren't interested. And what do you suppose Paul talked about? Paul talked to his guards about why he was there—and of course that was because of Jesus.

These Roman soldiers likely did their work in rotation. So Paul kept getting new guards, and he kept telling them the same story. In time everyone in that force of elite palace soldiers not only knew about Paul but about Jesus too!

As we learn in the book of Acts, Paul was also allowed to preach while he was under guard. "He welcomed all who came to see him," and "boldly and without hindrance he preached the kingdom of God" (Acts 28:30-31). "As a result," Paul writes, "it has become clear throughout the whole palace guard and to everyone else that I am in chains for Christ" (Phil. 1:13).

Paul made the most of every opportunity to serve Jesus (see Col. 4:5)! And many of the Christians in Rome respected him highly for that.

The Church in Rome—Support

One surprising—and seemingly ironic—result of Paul's imprisonment was that it brought encouragement; it helped to build up the church in Rome. Paul writes, "Because of my chains, most of the brothers in the Lord have been encouraged to speak the word of God more courageously and fearlessly" (Phil. 1:14). Why would that be so?

The answer is that these believers were inspired by Paul's example. The Christians who lived in Rome had heard about Paul shortly after his arrival among other prisoners. They quickly learned why he was there, and they talked about it among themselves. Some of them came to care for Paul as a brother in Christ, and large numbers of Jews and Jewish believers came to listen to him preach (Acts 28:12-24). Everyone could see that Paul, who was in chains though he "was not guilty of any crime deserving death" (28:18), was not only willing to be imprisoned for the gospel but also preached faithfully and boldly even while chained to his Roman guards. So why shouldn't the Christians in Rome spread the good news of Jesus faithfully and courageously too? They became fearless because of Paul's example as he served his Master by the power of God.

One of the reasons Paul is so thankful as he writes to the Philippians is that he has heard also of their faithfulness (Phil. 1:3-6). And he trusts that, like the fearless believers in Rome, they are contending "for the faith of the gospel without being frightened in any way by those who oppose" them (1:27-28). Through these words to his friends in Philippi, Paul is saying to all of us: *You do not have to feel intimidated anytime it becomes unpopular for you to be a Christian.*

The Church in Rome—Criticism

It soon became clear, though, that not all of the Christians in Rome supported him. Paul discovered that some of them were trying to "stir up trouble" for him while he was in chains (Phil. 1:17). Paul doesn't explain what these people had against him. He simply describes these people as preaching Christ "out of envy and rivalry" and "out of selfish ambition" (1:15, 17). They have unworthy motives in their way of preaching, doing it not out of "love" or "goodwill" (1:15-16).

How does Paul respond to these people? We might be surprised that he says, "What does it matter? The important thing is that in every way, whether from false motives or true, Christ is preached. And because of this I rejoice" (1:18).

In the face of this conflict Paul does not become defensive or resentful. After all, Paul is saying, they do believe in Jesus and proclaim him. Notice that Paul is not concerned about what these people think of him but only what they think of Jesus. Paul takes himself out of the equation, leaving Christ central.

Paul's response here is remarkable. Fellow believers in Christ are making trouble for him when they should be supporting him, and he says that this doesn't matter to him. It's as if Paul is saying, "Just forget it. Ignore it. Concentrate on the gospel. What counts is that they are still preaching Jesus." I wonder if I would be able to do the same under similar circumstances.

Additional Notes

1:6—"He who began a good work in you will carry it on to completion until the day of Christ Jesus." Paul wants the Philippian Christians to understand that God's kingdom work is much larger than that of any one person or local church and that it goes on forever. The kind of thing God is doing now through the ongoing spread of the gospel will continue into future generations as long as the world lasts, until "the day of Christ Jesus." We too need to recognize the importance of remaining faithful to the Lord whatever may happen, so the influence of the gospel may continue to prevail in this world.

1:11—"filled with the fruit of righteousness that comes through Jesus Christ—to the glory and praise of God." There are people who seem to think goodness (an aspect of "the fruit of righteousness") comes naturally and that Christianity hinders it. They are fond of pointing out all the failures of Christianity in history and all the faults of people who are Christians, saying that the church and religion and Christianity inhibit goodness. As Christians, we may candidly admit that we are still sinners and we have made mistakes, but we may not excuse ourselves. In Christ's name we are called to demonstrate "the fruit of righteousness," the "good life" that is possible only through faith in Jesus by the power of the Holy Spirit (see Gal. 5:22-25). And when we do, our lives give "the glory and praise" to God, who is behind it all.

1:13—"I am in chains for Christ." Sometimes we get the impression that nothing should go bad in our lives because we are Christians trying to serve the Lord. But that is seldom if ever true. Paul was serving the Lord faithfully, and yet he was in chains. When we ask, "Why is this bad thing happening to me?" it helps to remember that Jesus died on the cross for our sake, that Paul spent years in prison for the sake of the gospel, and that thousands of people have given their lives as Christian martyrs. We don't always have to understand why bad things happen to us; most important is that we remain faithful in all circumstances.

GENERAL DISCUSSION

1. Paul begins this letter with praise for the Philippian church (Phil. 1:3-6). In contrast, he begins his letter to the Galatian churches with criticism ("I am astonished that you are so quickly deserting the one who called you"—Gal. 1:6). What's the first thing that comes to mind when you think of your own church? Is it praise and thanksgiving, or criticism and judgment? How do you (or should you) balance these?

2. How can we tell if Christians are growing in God's love? (See Phil. 1:9-11.)

3. Put yourself in the place of a Roman soldier who was chained to Paul for a day. Describe some of the things you may have thought and how you may have felt about the situation.

4. Imagine being a Christian in Rome who had never heard of Paul before. How would you react when you heard the leaders of your church arguing about whether Paul was right or not? Would you be uninterested, curious, supportive, critical—or what? Explain.

5. Paul's statement "But what does it matter? . . ." may strike us as surprising. Does it really not matter what motives preachers have as they spread the gospel of Christ? Think of various kinds of preachers you've seen or heard about. Then try to sort out whether their message, though flawed, portrays the truth of the gospel.

SMALL GROUP SESSION IDEAS

Opening (10-15 minutes)

Pray—Thank the Lord for bringing you together again to study Scripture. Pray that each of you may benefit from the study and discussion of this lesson material. Try to incorporate something of the lesson content into your prayer—for example, "Lord, we pray that each of us may learn to respond to adversity the way Paul did, seeking first of all to focus on you and to bring glory to your name."

Share—At this point you may want to share briefly any thoughts or reactions that surprised you while studying the material for this lesson. You may also wish to talk about goals you may have set during the previous session, or about upcoming group projects you might like to do.

Focus—After observing Paul's reactions in the passage for this lesson, keep in mind the following question: *What does (or should) it mean to me to focus on Christ in all situations and to be concerned mainly with bringing glory to God?*

Growing (35-40 minutes)

Read—You may wish to read the Scripture passage for this lesson (along with portions of the study guide notes) before moving into your discussion time.

Discuss—Along with the General Discussion questions you may want to choose from the following process questions for additional reflection and discussion. You should feel free to respond openly or to reflect silently, as you wish, during any part of the discussion.

- Think about ways in which you've been able, in God's strength, to grow in love. For example, have you been able to grow in love for persons you once despised? Is getting along with other church members (or certain ones) hard for you at times? Why or why not? Without using the names of persons you may have in mind, share your thoughts with the rest of the group.

- When it comes to hearing the gospel preached, what has mattered more to you—has it perhaps been the delivery or the person delivering the message, or has it been the message itself? Reflect on ways in which God's truth has come through to you despite the shortcomings or faults of a preacher, and despite your own shortcomings or distractions as a listener. Share your thoughts with God and also with others in the group.

Goalsetting (5 minutes)

In response to the material for this session, try the following exercise sometime before you meet for your next session:

- Try to identify various and even conflicting responses about a major event that's happened recently. Maybe it was an important political election or convention. Maybe it was a tragic event such as a terrorist attack, a shooting spree, or a natural disaster. Maybe it was a crisis in your own church or community. Try to evaluate the responses you've heard or seen. Is one response more Christian than another? Why? How did (or might) you respond to the event? Pray about this, asking God for wisdom and insight. Pray also for wisdom on how to respond in any situation.

Closing (10-15 minutes)

Preparing for Prayer—Take some time to mention prayer requests you'd like to share, including personal praises and concerns as well as issues that may have come up during this session.

Prayer—Give thanks for the time you've been able to spend together in Bible study and for the working of the Holy Spirit in each of you. Ask for a unified spirit among you and in your church so that Christ's message may be proclaimed in line with God's will. Everyone may join in with prayer requests and praises. Also ask for wisdom as you seek to live for God's glory in light of things you've learned or rediscovered during this session.

Optional Singing—If you like singing together, you might like to try a song or two that picks up on a theme from this session, such as "The Church's One Foundation" or "Jesus, Name Above All Names."

*How do we go
about exalting
Christ?*

3

PHILIPPIANS 1:18-30

Christ Will Be Exalted

In a Nutshell

Paul's concern is that in all things Christ may be exalted. Why? Because Paul knows that the hope of the world, as well as the hope of every person, depends on Christ alone. The Spirit of Christ has the power to enable anyone to become the person God intends him or her to be. In our Scripture for this lesson Paul demonstrates true faith by affirming that he wants Christ to be exalted in his own life, whether he will be acquitted at his trial or condemned.

Philippians 1:18-30

[18]. . . The important thing is that in every way, whether from false motives or true, Christ is preached. And because of this I rejoice.

Yes, and I will continue to rejoice, [19]for I know that through your prayers and the help given by the Spirit of Jesus Christ, what has happened to me will turn out for my deliverance. [20]I eagerly expect and hope that I will in no way be ashamed, but will have sufficient courage so that now as always Christ will be exalted in my body, whether by life or by death. [21]For to me, to live is Christ and to die is gain. [22]If I am to go on living in the body, this will mean fruitful labor for me. Yet what shall I choose? I do not know! [23]I am torn between the two: I desire to depart and be with Christ, which is better by far; [24]but it is more necessary for you that I remain in the body. [25]Convinced of this, I know that I will remain, and I will continue with all of you for your progress and joy in the faith, [26]so that through my being with you again your joy in Christ Jesus will overflow on account of me.

[27]Whatever happens, conduct yourselves in a manner worthy of the gospel of Christ. Then, whether I come and see you or only hear about you in my absence, I will know that you stand firm in one spirit, contending as one man for the faith of the gospel [28]without being frightened in any way by those who oppose you. This is a sign to them that they will be destroyed, but that you will be saved—and that by God. [29]For it has been granted to you on behalf of Christ not only to believe on him, but also to suffer for him, [30]since you are going through the same struggle you saw I had, and now hear that I still have.

Paul's Expectation About His Trial

As we noted in lesson 2, Paul takes himself out of the equation so far as other people's preaching of Christ is concerned. Even if they preach from wrong motives that do injustice to Paul, the important thing is that Christ is being preached (Phil. 1:18). But now the apostle turns to focus on his own involvement as a servant of Christ, stating that he wants to remain faithful to the Lord, no matter what happens in his upcoming trial. Rejoicing in the support he has received through the Philippians' prayers and through "the Spirit of Jesus Christ" (1:19), Paul says, "I eagerly expect and hope that I will . . . have sufficient courage so that . . . Christ will be exalted in my body, whether by life or by death" (1:20).

Paul is realistic about his coming trial. He knows the verdict could go against him. Who knows how Nero will feel at the time—whether he will listen impartially to the evidence or deal unfairly with Paul? Whatever happens, says Paul, he is not afraid to die, because it "is better by far" to "depart and be with Christ" (1:23). Though he states that "to live is Christ," Paul makes clear that "to die is gain" (1:21).

Because he is "convinced" there is much "fruitful labor" ahead of him, however, Paul also makes clear that he expects to be acquitted (1:22, 25). "I know that I will remain," he states with conviction, "and I will continue with all of you for your progress and joy in the faith" (1:25). And this is the reason he gives: "It is more necessary for you that I remain in the body" (1:24). How truly Christ-centered Paul is! Though he would clearly choose "to depart and be with Christ," Paul indicates that his own "desire," even if it's a godly spiritual yearning, must not take top priority over God's will for him in the work of God's kingdom (1:22-23).

How many of us would be thinking like Paul if we were in his place? Would we be thinking it would be better to die and be with Christ than to go on living here? And would we be thinking about God's will for us over our own desires?

Again, Paul is more interested in what happens for the sake of the gospel than what happens to himself. He prays that "Christ will be exalted," whether that happens through Paul's life or through his death (1:20). That's pretty hard for a person to do, no matter what predicament he or she is in.

Worthy of the Gospel

We may notice in our Scripture for this lesson that Paul is not hesitant to talk about himself. After all, he knows the good Christians in Philippi are concerned about him. In some other letters Paul also takes considerable space to talk about his own situation or qualifications (for example, see 2 Cor. 10-12; Gal. 1-2).

But the apostle never leaves the attention centered on himself. "Whatever happens" to me, he writes, make sure you "conduct yourselves in a manner worthy of the gospel of Christ" (Phil. 1:27). If Paul is defending himself against his detractors, it's to assure his readers that what he has been preaching is indeed true (see 2 Cor. 10-12). If he is simply explaining what is happening to him, as here in Philippians 1, it's to encourage his readers to follow his example of faithfulness in the midst of hardship and persecution. *Make sure that you too,* Paul is saying, *keep your faith firm in the Lord and show it in your behavior.*

An underlying teaching here is that we are to show by our Christian living that we are indeed saved by the God of grace. Though our salvation is entirely the gift of God (1:28) and not in any way dependent on our good works, we must not think good works have nothing to do with salvation. James reminds us of this same teaching when he writes that "faith without deeds is dead" (James 2:26).

As believers in Christ, no matter what the circumstances, we are to act in a way that shows we truly believe in Jesus. Always and everywhere we are to be "worthy of the gospel," regardless of the reactions of others who may judge us negatively. We are called to live in such a way that "always Christ will be exalted" in our lives (Phil. 1:20). Each day we need to ask ourselves, *When God looks at us, does God see humble Christians doing their best to image Jesus in all they think, say, and do?*

Paul wants to hear and see, if possible, that the Christians in Philippi are continuing faithfully in the Christian life. "Then," he explains, "I will know that you stand firm in one spirit, contending as one man for the faith of the gospel without being frightened in any way by those who oppose you" (1:27-28).

Suffering with Paul (and Christ)

Paul adds that believers in Christ should not be surprised if they get into trouble because they are Christians. Paul reminds the Philippians that Jesus had to suffer and that Paul himself is suffering for the sake of Christ (1:30). Suffering for the sake of the gospel can be expected in Christian living. Paul explains: "It has been granted to you on behalf of Christ not only to believe on him, but also to suffer for him, since you are going through the same struggle you saw I had, and now hear that I still have" (1:29-30). We know, of course, that in those early centuries Christians had to go through a great deal of trouble because of their faith. This still happens in countries where Christianity begins to gain a foothold, and it happens (though usually to a lesser degree) in our modern, post-Christian society whenever we take a stand for Christ against false teachings and other influences of this world.

In our passage for this lesson Paul is encouraging the Philippian Christians to put their own times of persecution into perspective. While they struggle with what they are going through, it's good for them to look around and see what others also are going through—for example, Paul in his suffering for Christ as a prisoner in Rome. Paul has heard of their struggles with opposition, so he is mindful of their suffering (1:28-30). And he is encouraging them to be aware that they are not alone, just as he knows he is not alone, and that together they can strengthen each other in their suffering "on behalf of Christ" (1:29).

Underlying Paul's words of encouragement here is the broader teaching that both the Philippians and Paul—indeed, all believers—should also think of their suffering in comparison to Christ's. Jesus was crucified as a result of the Jewish leaders' cooperation with their Roman overlords. Paul is suffering because of legal trouble with both of these same groups, and he is also opposed by Christian rivals in Rome (1:15-17). It's likely that both Jews and Gentiles have been harassing the church in Philippi as well. But we must remember that Jesus shouldered far more suffering for our sake when he took upon himself the sins of all humanity and paid the price for them in our place (John 3:16). All of Jesus' suffering was unjust punishment so that we might be justified and saved to enjoy life in God's glorious presence forever.

In his earlier letter to the Christians in Rome, Paul says, "I consider that our present sufferings are not worth comparing with the glory that will be revealed in us" because of Christ (Rom. 8:18). Whenever he focuses on Christ in the context of suffering, Paul gives us a beautiful picture of finding sufficient strength to endure what he's going through (see 2 Cor. 1:3-7; 4:7-12; 6:3-10; 11:21-12:10; Phil. 4:10-20).

When we suffer for the sake of the gospel (that is, the "good news" of God's kingdom), we are sharing in the suffering of Jesus (see Mark 1:15). When we do that faithfully, Christ is exalted in us, whether we live or die.

Additional Notes

1:20—"I eagerly expect and hope that I will in no way be ashamed, but will have sufficient courage." Paul means "ashamed of the gospel" here. In other words, if pressured to renounce his faith in Jesus, Paul "eagerly expect[s]" that he would have the courage to stand and proclaim him Lord, "now as always" (1:20).

Another place where Paul mentions "eager expectation" is Romans 8:19—in reference to the creation's waiting for God's glory to be "revealed in us" (Rom. 8:18). When that happens, the creation (including our physical bodies) "will be liberated from its bondage to decay and brought into the glorious freedom of the children of God" (8:21; see 1 Cor. 15:35-58). Paul may well have this same idea in mind as he writes to the Philippians about his expectations while suffering "in chains for Christ" (Phil. 1:13, 19-30). Scholars have noted that the word *apokaradokia*—used only in Romans 8:19 and Philippians 1:20—may even have been coined by Paul to refer to "a state of keen anticipation of the future, the craning of the neck to catch a glimpse of what lies ahead" (*Tyndale New Testament Commentaries: The Epistle of Paul to the Philippians*, p. 75).

"Christ will be exalted in my body." How is Christ exalted in our bodies? By what we do with them, remembering that each of us is a body-soul unity. If we do our daily work conscientiously as believers in Christ, we honor Christ with our bodies, exalting him. If we compromise our faith in Jesus by acting in ways inconsistent with God's will for us, we dishonor Christ with our bodies. As Paul reminds the Corinthians, every believer's body is a "temple of the Holy Spirit" (1 Cor. 6:19-20), so whatever we do with our bodies must be consistent with our walk with God. All we think, say, and do takes place in relation to our bodies, in which the Spirit of God lives (3:16). Here in Philippians 1:20 Paul is saying that he wants to live every day in faithful obedience to Christ, and that even if he must die, he wants to do so without denying Christ in his suffering.

1:23—"I am torn between the two." Paul is torn between wanting to go on living and spreading the gospel, and wanting to die to be with Christ. I wonder how many of us would be torn by such a dilemma. Death is still such a fearsome enemy to us that it's highly unusual—even unnatural—not to fear dying. Paul's "desire," though, is to "be with Christ," so he's looking far beyond death to the joy of living in blessedness and peace (*shalom*) in God's presence. Paul may well have feared death as much as any of us do, but for him, because of Christ, death had lost its "sting" (1 Cor. 15:55-57)—the threat of eternal punishment for sin. With Christ's victory in mind, we too may trust our Lord to use death as a doorway to bring us into eternal life in his presence.

1:26—"Through my being with you again your joy in Christ Jesus will overflow on account of me." In this expression, which may sound rather unusual to us, Paul is saying, in effect, "I want to make you all very happy in Jesus; I will do this by coming to visit you after I am released from prison. When you see me alive, you will be overflowing with joy in Christ."

1:27—"Stand firm in one spirit, contending as one man for the faith of the gospel." Amid all the denominations of Christian churches, this teaching of Paul can be hard to remember. Sometimes we overlook the basic fact that all Christians should be standing as one person for the gospel of Christ, who is our one Head (Eph. 4:15). We must remember, as Paul says to the Ephesians, that "there is one body and one Spirit . . . one Lord, one faith, one baptism; one God and Father of all, who is over all and through all and in all" (4:4-6). Our petty squabbles sometimes loom larger than they really are. There is only one Spirit of Christ, and that Spirit animates and lives in all Christians.

1:28—"without being frightened in any way by those who oppose you. This is a sign to them that they will be destroyed." Many anti-Christian powers operate in this world, and they sometimes intimidate Christians, who become fearful to admit they are followers of Christ. But Paul indicates that the very fact that Christians can stand in God's power and not be frightened by anti-Christian forces is a warning that opposition to the gospel cannot succeed. This actually happened to a large extent in the later Roman persecutions against Christianity (begun by Nero around A.D. 65). Many people became converts when they saw or heard how faithful Christians were, unafraid to be executed or to face lions in the amphitheater. As one ancient church father expressed it, "The blood of the martyrs is the seed of the church."

1:30—"You are going through the same struggle you saw I had, and now hear that I still have." Paul appears to be mentioning three different situations of suffering here: (1) some sort of persecution continuing in Philippi, causing difficulties for the Christians there; (2) the struggle Paul and Silas had originally when they first came to the city and were imprisoned (Acts 16:16- 40); (3) the problem that has brought Paul to Rome (see lesson 1). In one way or another we are all called not only to believe but also to continue in faith despite opposition and the sufferings it may bring.

GENERAL DISCUSSION

1. Paul was not afraid to die. Are you? Why or why not?

2. Recall a time when you were seriously ill, say, enough to be hospitalized. What was uppermost in your mind—that Christ be exalted or that you get well?

3. Paul urges the Philippian Christians, "Conduct yourselves in a manner worthy of the gospel of Christ" (Phil. 1:27). What's the connection between faith in Jesus and living a good life—that is, living in a way that's worthy of being called a Christian?

4. Paul regards it as a gift or privilege to suffer for Christ (Phil. 1:29). What kind of suffering is suffering for Christ? In what ways do people suffer for Christ today?

5. Has there been a time when you experienced a lot of self-pity and then found relief when comparing your suffering to the Lord's? Share your thoughts with the rest of the group.

SMALL GROUP SESSION IDEAS

Opening (10-15 minutes)

Pray—As you begin your session together, thank the Lord for the blessings of daily life, and pray for continued faithfulness even in times of difficulty and sorrow. Pray also for the guidance of the Holy Spirit, who leads us "into all truth" (John 16:13). We need to be open to the Spirit's instruction, even if it means changing our opinion about something or our ways of doing things. Try to incorporate something of today's lesson into your prayer by saying, for example, "Lord, help us all to live each day and in all circumstances in a way that brings glory to your name."

Share—Talk with each other about goals you may have set, project ideas you might like to try (see group projects at the end of this session), or something you may have learned while preparing for this session. Keep this sharing time brief, using it to help each other focus again on Philippians and to "get into" the material for this session.

Focus—Try to focus on the following question throughout this session: *In tough times, do I conduct myself in a way that's consistent with my faith in Jesus? If not, what can I do to be more faithful?*

Growing (35-40 minutes)

Read—If you like reading the Scripture passage during your session, you might have two people cover the reading: one for Philippians 1:18-26, and the other for 1:27-30. You may also want to read or review sections of the study guide notes or leader's notes before moving into your discussion time.

Discuss—As you work through the General Discussion questions (see especially questions 1-4), you may want to include the following process questions for additional reflection and discussion:

- Think of a time when you were in a really tough predicament. Maybe even your life was on the line. What was your greatest concern? Did it have anything to do with glorifying God? Why or why not? Would you react or respond any differently today? Share your thoughts with the rest of the group.

- Do you know (of) anyone who's been persecuted for being a Christian—thrown in jail, beaten, or even martyred? Reflect together on what it can mean to stand up for Christ in a world that's hostile to his claims—even in our "comfortable" Western society.

Goalsetting (5 minutes)

In response to this session, try to accomplish one or both of the following goals:

- I need to reflect on ways in which I can be more like Paul (and Christ) in being prepared to die. I want to pray regularly about this and be open to the Spirit's leading and Christ's comforting power. Here's what I'd like to pray:

- I want to be able to conduct myself in a way that's worthy of Christ, in any and every situation. So I pledge to pray each day for the Lord's help in doing this. Here's what I'd like to pray:

Closing (10-15 minutes)

Preparing for Prayer—Share praises, concerns, and other matters you'd like to bring before God in prayer. Be sure to mention any goals you may be working on in relation to this study of Philippians, as well as any important issues that have come up during this session.

Prayer—One way to do your closing prayer this time might be to try simple, one-sentence prayers. It's OK, as well, to have times of silence. As a group, this is your time to be in conversation together with God, who cares about all our concerns and listens to all we have to say. As you pray together, ask the Lord to help each one of you live faithfully every day by glorifying God in all you do and living in a way that's worthy of the gospel.

Optional Singing—If you like to sing, you might close with a song that touches on one or more of the themes of this session, such as "O Master, Let Me Walk with Me" or "Create in Me a Clean Heart, O God."

Group Study Project (Optional)

Some of you may be interested in learning more about believers who've suffered or who've been martyred for Christ. A couple of places to start would be with *The New Foxe's Book of Martyrs* (2001 edition) and *Jesus Freaks: dc Talk and the Voice of the Martyrs* (1999), available at most Christian bookstores or in libraries.

After researching the topic, perhaps you could summarize what you've learned or give a few readings about persecuted Christians during your next session, which focuses on our unity with Christ in both his humiliation and his exaltation. Or, if you need more time, you could make your presentation during a later session (for example, session 5, which touches again on Paul's being a prisoner, or session 8, which focuses on contentment in times of need and suffering.)

*How can we
imitate Jesus'
attitude?*

4

United with Christ

In a Nutshell

Paul wants to encourage his friends in Philippi to persevere in the faith. He wants to explain the implications of committing their lives to Jesus as Lord. So at this point in his letter the apostle emphasizes that they must maintain their unity with Christ and that they should do so by imitating Jesus' attitude. Jesus' attitude of humility toward life in general is the pattern all Christians should follow in their lives. And here Paul describes what that pattern is like.

Philippians 2:1-11

¹If you have any encouragement from being united with Christ, if any comfort from his love, if any fellowship with the Spirit, if any tenderness and compassion, ²then make my joy complete by being like-minded, having the same love, being one in spirit and purpose. ³Do nothing out of selfish ambition or vain conceit, but in humility consider others better than yourselves. ⁴Each of you should look not only to your own interests, but also to the interests of others.

⁵Your attitude should be the same as that of Christ Jesus:

⁶Who, being in very nature God,
did not consider equality with God
something to be grasped,

⁷but made himself nothing,
taking the very nature of a servant,
being made in human likeness.
⁸And being found in appearance as a man,
he humbled himself
and became obedient to death—even
death on a cross!
⁹Therefore God exalted him to the highest
place
and gave him the name that is above
every name,
¹⁰that at the name of Jesus every knee
should bow,
in heaven and on earth and under the
earth,
¹¹and every tongue confess that Jesus
Christ is Lord,
to the glory of God the Father.

Union with Christ Includes Union with Christians

Look at what Paul says here about "being united with Christ": in Christ you have "encouragement," "comfort," "fellowship with the Spirit," "tenderness," and "compassion" (Phil. 2:1).

As Christians, we must be careful not to think that just believing in Jesus is enough. Faith has to carry over into life.

So in this brief statement (half of a sentence!) Paul lists several characteristics we acquire if our faith is sincere. We are not negative, defeated, or pessimistic. We can be encouraged and comforted even if troubles surround us. And we enjoy all this by means of fellowship with the very Spirit who unites us "with Christ," empowering us to be tender and compassionate—like Christ.

Paul would not agree with people today who insist that one's faith is a private matter. In fact, he insists that Christians must always remember they are part of a group, the body of Christ, the church. Paul tells his friends in Philippi that they must try hard to be "like-minded," loving each other, "being one in spirit and purpose" (2:2). Christians must not be "selfish," pushing themselves ahead, or "conceited"; instead they should be humble, putting others ahead of themselves (2:3). "Each of you," he says, "should look not only to your own interests, but also to the interests of others" (2:4). He knows there are some differences of opinion in the Philippian church (see 4:2-3), but those differences should not be allowed to destroy the Philippians' sense of unity in Christ Jesus or to interfere with the progress of the gospel.

"Being united with Christ" means being united with everyone else who is also "united with Christ" (2:1). We sometimes watch Christians split away from their congregation because of some dispute. They form a new church that does not keep fellowship with the previous one. Sometimes the dispute is bitter and caustic with the result that mutual respect is gone. This ought not to happen.

We can't possibly get away from our fellow believers in Jesus. How can we escape the others who believe in the same Lord we do? Who would want to?

Paul encourages us to be "like-minded." But even when we are not, we need to be careful not to despise the persons with whom we may disagree. We are still brothers and sisters in the Lord.

Jesus' Example

What attitude should we have about being a Christian? Not one of self-expression or self-realization. Not one in which we think of ourselves primarily as Lutheran, Calvinist, Baptist, Roman Catholic, Episcopal, or Methodist. We should have the same attitude Jesus had. Paul writes, "Your attitude should be the same as that of Christ Jesus" (2:5). It should be more important for us to be united with Christ and with others through Christ than to be in one particular denomination or church affiliation. We may well think a Reformed or Lutheran or Presbyterian view of things is better than Roman Catholic or Pentecostal or whatever, but that should not obscure the fact that others are also Christians. Just as we are to be united with Christ in our local church body, we are also to be united with believing Christians in other churches and denominations.

There were no denominations yet in Paul's day, but before long some disputes and divisions began to take place because of false teachings (heresies such as Gnosticism). It was hundreds of years, though, before any major splits began to occur. So the situation we have today is much different. Still, nothing should obscure the fact that Christians are all admonished to find their pattern of life in Jesus, not in any church leader or any church organization. It surely must be confusing for new Christians to discover that there are numerous competing groups all calling themselves Christian! Even so, it is possible for us in different church organizations to respect one another as part of the same "fellowship with the Spirit."

Each one of us needs to remember that first and foremost we must be true to Christ. We don't first look to our inner thoughts and attitudes and then make Christianity fit ourselves. We first get to know Jesus and his attitude, and then we shape our own character and opinions in line with Christ. This is an extremely important point to understand—especially today, when we are bombarded by individualism and division on every side.

Jesus' Attitude of Humility

What, then, is the attitude of Christ Jesus that we need to imitate? Jesus was "in very nature God," but he did not insist on being treated as God (2:6). Instead he took on "the very nature of a servant" (2:7). And in that nature, "in human likeness," he "humbled himself" as far as a human person could, even "to death" (2:7-8).

How do we imitate that attitude? By not acting as if we were our own God, as if we could take the place of God in our lives. A person who acts that way insists, "This is what I want, and I'm going to have it—no matter what. These are my goals in life, and I'll do anything and everything to achieve them—whatever it takes. I'm running my own life."

That, as we can see, is the opposite of being like Jesus. Jesus not only accepted his human existence willingly, becoming dependent on his Father in heaven, which was like becoming "nothing" after setting aside the glory of being God (2:6-7). He also allowed himself to be treated like dirt—and without complaining. That may well be more than most of us are willing to do. Be human? Yes. Obey God? Yes. But be treated unjustly and unfairly without complaining? Well . . .

Paul is telling the Philippian Christians that since Jesus humbled himself even to death—"even death on a cross," the most humiliating, cursed death a person could be sentenced with (Gal. 3:13), and for our sake!—then we should be willing to follow his example. Paul knows that the Philippians' persecution might get more severe than any they have experienced so far. And they should not complain, he says, but follow Jesus' example, adopting his attitude toward it. As followers of Christ, they must even be willing to die for his sake.

Most of us in Western civilization have not been challenged to that extent. But how would it be for you if you lived in another country and people burned down your house because you were a Christian? How would you react?

Jesus' Exaltation

It's illuminating to note God's response to the obedience of Christ. "Therefore God exalted him to the highest place," Paul writes, referring to the resurrection and ascension of Jesus (Phil. 2:9). This means God exalted Jesus as a human being to rule in heaven over all things in heaven and on earth (Eph. 1:2-23)!

And what does that mean? It means no less than that Jesus is exercising the full power of God everywhere. Or, to put it another way, God the Father is now exercising control of all things through the Son of God, Jesus. And since God the Holy Spirit came on Pentecost to fill Jesus' followers with new life in Christ, Jesus is with us always, just as he promised before he ascended to heaven (Matt. 28:18-20; John 16:7-15; Acts 1:8-11; 2:1-4).

God has given "all authority [power] in heaven and on earth" to Jesus (Matt. 28:18), and Jesus will remain with his followers through the gift of the Holy Spirit to the end of time. Paul wants the Philippian Christians to understand that no matter what happens to them, Jesus is in control of what happens all around them. Paul is telling the Philippians and us that all history now and always will be controlled and dominated by Christ Jesus. God controls life and history precisely by the power and working of the Spirit of Christ and by the Spirit-led spread of the gospel of Christ. We need to understand that God's power is the decisive force operating in the world around us, now as ever.

Paul insists therefore that "at the name of Jesus every knee should bow . . . and every tongue confess that Jesus Christ is Lord, to the glory of God the Father" (Phil. 2:10-11). Every being "in heaven and on earth and under the earth" is subject to the rule of Christ (2:10). For us in particular this means everybody in the whole world! That's the goal of the gospel.

Think about how far the gospel has spread since Paul wrote these words. Think also about how much farther it needs to spread.

Is all this realistic? Can you even conceive of a world in which everyone confesses "that Jesus Christ is Lord"? By the power of God this is possible. This is our Lord's goal, and we, "being united with Christ" (2:1), need to live in such a way that this goal may be promoted. We need to live like Jesus, beginning with humility.

Additional Notes

2:2—"Make my joy complete. . . ." The Philippians have already given Paul joy by sending him gifts and support through Epaphroditus (2:25; 4:18). And now he is saying, in effect, *Give me the additional joy of knowing you are fulfilling your calling of "being one in spirit and purpose," humble, and unselfish, showing love and care for one another in Christ. Then my joy will be complete.*

2:5-7—"Your attitude should be the same as that of Christ Jesus." Just as Jesus humbled himself and accepted "the very nature of a servant," we need to accept whatever position in life God puts us in, whether high or low in the estimation of society in general.

2:9—"the name that is above every name." Notice the irony here. Jesus might feasibly have set up a new kingdom of the Jews that ruled over all others, with himself as the highest official, the greatest king. The devil had even tempted him to do so (Luke 4:5-8). But he chose not to, and in the end God exalted him even higher than he might have been. And one day everyone "in heaven and on earth and under the earth" will "confess that Jesus Christ is Lord" (2:10-11). You can't get any higher than that!

GENERAL DISCUSSION

1. Paul lists several things in Philippians 2:1-3 that should characterize the Christian life. Examine the effects that being a Christian has had on your own life (for example, learning to control your temper, learning to appreciate people who have more talent than you, being content even when circumstances are unfavorable, and so on). In your own judgment, which effects are most valuable to you?

2. Paul says we should be "one in spirit and purpose" (Phil. 2:2). Since Christians around the world now belong to many different churches or denominations, some of which disagree with each other, how can we strive toward this goal?

3. Paul writes that "in humility" we should "consider others better" than ourselves (Phil. 2:3). What exactly does this mean?

4. What is the attitude of Jesus that Paul says we should imitate? What practical difference does that make in your life?

5. What does it mean that God exalted Jesus "to the highest place" (Phil. 2:9)?

6. In what ways does Jesus exercise the power of God within the world we live in? How does this work out in our lives?

SMALL GROUP SESSION IDEAS

Opening (10-15 minutes)

Pray—As you open this session with prayer, ask that God's will be done on earth among us, that we may serve in Christlike humility. Thank God for sending Jesus to save us and to show us how to live to the glory of God. Ask that the Lord will keep us faithful in times of difficulty and keep us humble as we seek to persevere in faith.

Share—Take a few moments to share questions or surprises you may have encountered in the material for this lesson. You may also want to talk about goals or group projects you've decided to do.

Focus—Try to keep the following questions in mind through-out this session: *How do I imitate Jesus in my life? In what areas can I improve? How do we as a group or as a church imitate Jesus?*

Growing (35-40 minutes)

Read—If you like to read the Scripture together before your discussion time, the passage for this lesson again divides easily into two parts: Philippians 2:1-4 and 2:5-11. If you like, you could divide the song in 2:5-11 into two parts as well: 2:5-8 on Jesus' humiliation and 2:9-11 on Jesus' exaltation. You may also wish to review portions of the study guide notes.

Discuss—If you'd like to insert some process questions for additional personal reflection and discussion as you work through the General Discussion questions, you might try the following (or include some of your own):

- Think of someone who's modeled the example of Christlike humility by showing tenderness and compassion with the goal of building up the body of Christ (unity). What was the situation? Did the experience help you grow closer to God? Explain.

- Think of people you know (of) who have shown good stewardship or servanthood in terms of influencing our society and/or world as a result of the transforming power of Christ the exalted King (for example, through leadership, invention, science, art, business, and so on). Share an example or two with the rest of the group, focusing on how their contributions give glory to God.

Goalsetting (5 minutes)

Perhaps one concrete thing that everyone could do in the coming week is to observe other Christians and try to identify

41

examples of believers who glorify God by helping others at a real cost to themselves.

Closing (10-15 minutes)

Preparing for Prayer—Take some time to offer comfort, tenderness, and compassion to each other, if needed, by sharing concerns and praises you'd like to bring before God in prayer. Also mention goals or group projects you may be working on.

Prayer—Thank God again for the great gift of Jesus, who made the gift of salvation possible for us. Give thanks also for people empowered by Christ who have helped others at a considerable cost to themselves for the sake of God's glory. Everyone may join in with additional concerns and praises. Ask the Spirit of God to fill each one of you with more and more Christlike humility and to help you contribute to Christ's rule in this world each day.

Optional Singing or Reading—If you'd like, you could include some singing or reading as you close this session. Some songs that fit with themes of this session are "Make Me a Channel of Your Peace," "Spirit of the Living God," and "Lead Me, Guide Me."

For a reading you could try Psalm 25:4-10 or the following lines from *Our World Belongs to God: A Contemporary Testimony* (st. 51-52):

> In our work, even in dull routine,
> we hear the call to serve our Lord.
> We must work for more than wages,
> and manage for more than profit,
> so that mutual respect
> and the just use of goods and skills
> may shape the work place,
> and so that, while we earn or profit,
> useful products and services may result.

> Grateful for the advances
> in science and technology,
> we make careful use of their products,
> on guard against idolatry
> and harmful research,
> and careful to use them in ways that answer
> to God's demands
> to love our neighbor
> and to care for the earth and its creatures.

*How does God
work within
us?*

5

PHILIPPIANS 2:12-30

Working Out Salvation

In a Nutshell
We need to work at our salvation, but as we do, we must realize God is working in us at the same time. Why do some people want to be Christians? Because God is at work in them. God's work in us can be seen precisely in what we want to do and to be.

Philippians 2:12-30
[12]Therefore, my dear friends, as you have always obeyed—not only in my presence, but now much more in my absence—continue to work out your salvation with fear and trembling, [13]for it is God who works in you to will and to act according to his good purpose.

[14]Do everything without complaining or arguing, [15]so that you may become blameless and pure, children of God without fault in a crooked and depraved generation, in which you shine like stars in the universe [16]as you hold out the word of life—in order that I may boast on the day of Christ that I did not run or labor for nothing. [17]But even if I am being poured out like a drink offering on the sacrifice and service coming from your faith, I am glad and rejoice with all of you. [18]So you too should be glad and rejoice with me.

[19]I hope in the Lord Jesus to send Timothy to you soon, that I also may be cheered when I receive news about you. [20]I have no one else like him, who takes a genuine interest in your welfare. [21]For everyone looks out for his own interests, not those of Jesus Christ. [22]But you know that Timothy has proved himself, because as a son with his father he has served with me in the work of the gospel. [23]I hope, therefore, to send him as soon as I see how things go with me. [24]And I am confident in the Lord that I myself will come soon.

[25]But I think it is necessary to send back to you Epaphroditus, my brother, fellow worker and fellow soldier, who is also your messenger, whom you sent to take care of my needs. [26]For he longs for all of you and is distressed because you heard he was ill. [27]Indeed he was ill, and almost died. But God had mercy on him, and not on him only but also on me, to spare me sorrow upon sorrow. [28]Therefore I am all the more eager to send him, so that when you see him again you may be glad and I may have less anxiety. [29]Welcome him in the Lord with great joy, and honor men like him, [30]because he almost died for the work of Christ, risking his life to make up for the help you could not give me.

Work Out Your Salvation

Christians need to imitate Jesus, says Paul (as we discussed in lesson 4), and that means adopting Jesus' attitude toward God and life.

How do we do that? Paul urges the Philippians—and us—with these thought-provoking words: "Continue to work out your salvation with fear and trembling" (Phil. 2:12). Faith needs to carry over into personal life—goals, ambitions, character, habits, relationships, work, family life, social conduct, and all the rest. It's a beautiful thing to see a Christian striving to really *live* by faith in the power of God each day. But what a sad thing it is to see a Christian who refuses to work at being the best person he or she can be.

Paul goes on to explain: "It is God who works in you to will and to act according to his good purpose" (2:13). So we need to understand that to work at our salvation does not mean we save ourselves; it means we recognize that God is at work in us, by means of the Holy Spirit, and that we are responding. It means we are being obedient to God, just as Jesus was.

To believe in Jesus is to be disciplined by him by means of God's Word and Spirit. Paul explains further to his Philippian friends what it means to work out their salvation: "Do everything without complaining or arguing, so that you may become blameless and pure, children of God without fault in a crooked and depraved generation" (2:14-15). Christians in those days were a tiny minority as they tried to be blameless and pure amid the depravity of the culture they lived in. They needed to show in their everyday interactions with people that they were somehow different, filled with the love and light of God, who straightens out the crooked places in people's lives. And they could do this by living in line with the Spirit of God, who was busy at work in them.

Notice that Paul is describing here what happens to our character because we are Christians. Each of us becomes the kind of person Jesus was. Each becomes a person with a heart close to God, a person united with God (2:1).

While we are not saved by our actions, our actions are evidence that we are saved and living in union with God. The closer we come to be like Christ, the more obvious it is that we are truly Christians (Luke 6:43-45). As we all know, though, some people can go to church and do many other things that give the impression of being a Christian while covering up a life of sin. But sooner or later their hypocrisy comes out or gives way to repentance (John 3:19-21; 1 Cor. 3:11- 15; 4:5; Eph. 5:8-14).

Our world is vastly different from the Roman world of Paul's day. We live in a culture shaped largely by Christian faith and values. But the words of Paul still remind us that we need to know how to live as Christians when social conditions contradict truth, goodness, and purity. In this world Christian struggle (and growth!) will continue. Even after we die, our children and grandchildren must carry on as God works in and through them (Phil. 2:12-13).

When Paul thought of his Philippian friends continuing to serve the Lord in faith, shining "like stars in the universe" as they held out "the word of life," this gave him great joy (2:15-17). Like Paul, we need to keep trusting that the day of great glory will come, when "every knee" will bow and "every tongue confess that Jesus Christ is Lord" (2:10-11).

Timothy

At this point in his letter Paul moves on to talk about Timothy, perhaps because this young assistant is a good example of a believer who shines like a star as he holds out "the word of life" (2:15-16).

Paul tells the Philippians that he intends to send Timothy to them soon. Why? Apparently to let them know what happens during his upcoming trial. He writes, "I hope . . . to send him as soon as I see how things go with me" (2:23).

Who was Timothy? He was one of Paul's associates who traveled with him on some of his missionary journeys. Usually Paul had several people with him; various New Testament passages mention Silas, Luke, Titus, Timothy, Mark, and others. Paul would sometimes also send these assistants on side trips to visit a church here and there when he was unable to go (see Acts 19:22; 20:4-5).

Timothy was born and raised in Lystra, one of the cities Paul visited on his first missionary journey with Barnabas (14:8, 21; 16:1). It seems that Timothy, still quite young, came to believe in Christ as a result of that visit. His mother, who was Jewish, was a believer by the time Paul came back to visit Lystra on his second missionary journey, and Timothy's father "was a Greek"—which may mean he was Greek by birth or simply that he was a Gentile (16:1). There's evidence that Timothy's grandmother Lois, the mother of Eunice (his mother), was a believer also (2 Tim. 1:5). When Paul passed through Lystra again on his second missionary journey, Timothy joined him. From then on, Timothy remained a faithful missionary associate of Paul.

It's interesting to note that Paul had Timothy circumcised when he joined the missionary team. Apparently Timothy's Greek background, which meant he was not circumcised, could have caused some trouble for Paul among Jews in the area as he and the missionary team went about their work (Acts 16:3). (Paul himself got into big trouble later in Jerusalem when some Jews thought he was bringing a Gentile into the temple there. That trouble, as we discussed in lesson 1, led up to the situation Paul was in now as a prisoner in Rome—see Acts 21:27-32.) Still, it's intriguing that Paul, who often preached against forcing Gentiles to be circumcised (1 Cor. 7:17-20; Gal. 5:1-12; Phil. 3:2-4), had this operation performed on Timothy. Most scholars reason that Paul was applying here the principle of not being a stumbling block to others so that, by God's grace, he might be able to bring the message of salvation most effectively. In 1 Corinthians 9:19-22 Paul explains this principle this way:

> Though I am free and belong to no man, I make myself a slave to everyone, to win as many as possible. To the Jews I became like a Jew, to win the Jews. To those under the law I became like one under the law (though I myself am not under the law), so as to win those under the law. To those not having the law I became like one not having the law (though I am not free from God's law but am under Christ's law), so as to win those not having the law. To the weak I became weak, to win the weak. I have become all things to all men so that by all possible means I might save some.

This Timothy is the same person to whom Paul later wrote two letters (1 and 2 Timothy). Sometime after his imprisonment in Rome, Paul apparently sent Timothy, who was still a young man, to be a temporary pastor in Ephesus, where he was when Paul wrote those letters to provide some pastoral guidance.

Now, though, while Paul is in prison in Rome and writing to the Philippians, Timothy is with him, probably seeing to his needs and keeping him informed about what others are saying about him (Phil. 1:14-18). Timothy is also waiting to bring word to the Philippians (and probably others) about the outcome of Paul's trial before Caesar (2:23).

Epaphroditus

We do not know much about Epaphroditus, other than what we can deduce from Paul's letter to the Philippians. He was not a member of Paul's missionary team; he was a helper sent from the church in Philippi. On behalf of the church there, he delivered gifts to help Paul with expenses and other needs while under house arrest in Rome (2:25; 4:18), as we have noted in previous lessons. Paul describes him also as a "brother, fellow worker and fellow soldier" (2:25).

Epaphroditus therefore must have been a highly trusted member of the church in Philippi, possibly even an elder (or "overseer"—see 1:1). Perhaps he thought he might remain in Rome until Paul's trial, and then be able to bring news back when he returned. But while he was in Rome, Epaphroditus became deathly sick (2:26-27). Paul adds, "He almost died for the work of Christ, risking his life to make up for the help you could not give me" (2:30).

After Epaphroditus recovered, Paul thought it would be best for him to return to Philippi without waiting any longer. "He longs for all of you and is distressed because you heard he was ill," Paul explains (2:26). "But God had mercy on him," says Paul, "and not on him only but also on me, to spare me sorrow upon sorrow" (1:27). It surely would have added to Paul's sorrow in prison if this helpful gift-bearer had died before finishing his mission of mercy on Paul's behalf. "Therefore," Paul says, "I am all the more eager to send him, so that when you see him again you may be glad and I may have less anxiety" (2:28).

Together with Paul we can thank the Lord for people like Timothy and Epaphroditus. They are both good examples of how Christians go about working out their salvation as God works in them "to will and to act according to his good purpose" (2:13).

Additional Notes

2:17—"poured out like a drink offering." Paul is picturing himself here in terms of the religious custom of pouring out a little wine on a sacrifice—a libation—in honor of God (Gen. 35:14; Ex. 29:38-41; 30:9; Lev. 23:13, 18). Many pagan religions used libations in their rituals also (see Ps. 16:4; Jer. 44:15-23). Paul uses this analogy to describe what his death (if it came as a result of his trial) would be like. His death would be like a libation poured out in honor of the Lord Jesus (see also 2 Tim. 4:6).

2:20—"I have no one else like him." High praise for a young assistant! We do not know much about Timothy's personal skills and abilities, but we can tell that Paul values Timothy very highly, treating him as a father would his own son. In the meantime Timothy is learning how to be a pastor, an evangelist, and a preacher as a protégé of Paul—learning while doing. In some ways we might compare this situation to the many people who train for work in ministry today by doing internships and ministry assignments while completing important course work.

GENERAL DISCUSSION

1. When Paul writes, "Continue to work out your salvation with fear and trembling" (Phil. 2:12), does he mean that we earn our salvation by doing good or that we let our salvation be seen by doing good? Explain.

2. Paul also writes, "It is God who works in you to will and to act according to his good purpose" (Phil. 2:13). Explain what this means.

3. Is it realistic for Paul to write, ". . . so that you may become blameless and pure, children of God without fault" (Phil. 2:15)? Are you, for example, without fault? Explain.

4. Paul describes the Roman world as "a crooked and depraved generation" (Phil. 2:15). Would you describe our world today in the same way? Why or why not?

SMALL GROUP SESSION IDEAS

Opening (10-15 minutes)

Pray—As you open with prayer, ask for the Lord's help as you work out your salvation in the way you live each day, and give thanks to God for working in your lives in such a way that you really want to serve. Pray always from the point of view of desiring that God's will may be done in us and in this world.

Share—Talk with each other briefly about how you're doing on goals you may have set during previous sessions. You could also take a few moments to reflect together on teachings in Philippians that may sound new or confusing to you.

Focus—During this session try to bear in mind the following focus questions: *What does it mean for me to work out my salvation? What does it mean for us as a group? As a church?*

Growing (35-40 minutes)

Read—You can read Philippians 2:12-30 together during your session time, if you like, by having four people read the four paragraphs: 2:12-13, 14-18, 19-24, 25-30. You may also wish to read or review sections of the study guide notes.

Discuss—As you work through the General Discussion questions, you may want to use the following process questions for additional personal reflection and discussion:

- Share your personal thoughts about what Paul means as he writes, "Work out your salvation with fear and trembling, for it is God who works in you . . ." (Phil. 2:12-13). Compare these words to Galatians 5:6; Ephesians 2:8-10; James 2:22, 26; 1 John 3:16-20. Do these passages help to clarify what Paul is saying here? Explain.

- Think of people you know (of) who are like Timothy and Epaphroditus. In what ways have these people helped to strengthen your faith? Share your thoughts with the rest of the group.

Goalsetting (5 minutes)

Perhaps everyone could agree on setting a group goal this time, focusing on something concrete from the Scripture passage, such as "Do everything without complaining or arguing" (Phil. 2:14). For example, you could try to see how often you can catch yourself complaining or arguing in the course of a day or a week. One way to do this could be to set a goal of reflecting three or four times each day—say, at meal times and at the end of the day—and jotting a note about each time you complained or fussed or whined or argued or got short-tempered or whatever. Also be sure to pray, asking the Spirit to help you see when you are complaining and what you can do about it. For many of us, complaining can become so natural that we seldom realize we are doing it!

Closing (10-15 minutes)

Preparing for Prayer—Share personal concerns, praises, and other requests that you'd like to bring to the Lord in prayer. Also feel free to mention goals or group projects you may be working on.

Prayer—Take turns praying as the Spirit moves you, either about something mentioned while preparing for prayer or about something else that calls for prayer. It's OK also to have times of silence and silent prayer in between spoken prayers. Then, if you'd like, you could conclude by saying the Lord's Prayer together.

Optional Singing—If you like singing together, you could include a song that fits one or more of the themes of this session, such as "I Sought the Lord, and Afterward I Knew," "The Lord Is My Light and My Salvation," or "The Servant Song."

Group Service Project (Optional)

Some or all of you may be interested in a service project that gives you an opportunity to show the Lord's work in your lives as you "work out your salvation" (Phil. 2:12). You could check with health, welfare, political action, denominational, and environmental agencies for ideas and for help in getting started. Be creative! Follow the Lord's leading to do something that can make an impact for Christ in your community and beyond.

For example, you might help in a local immunization clinic, a blood drive, or a food program. Or you could clean up a roadway, waterway, or disaster site. You could help with house renovation or new-home building projects. You could also get involved in legal justice, anti-racism, or community safety. Or you could work with literacy and basic-skills education, biblical literacy, acceptance and education of mentally impaired persons, responsible medical research, preservation of wildlife, proper use of land, purification of air and water, and much more.

We can "hold out the word of life" in every area of our lives as we "confess that Jesus Christ is Lord, to the glory of God" (2:11, 16). Our King and Savior calls us to seek God's kingdom and righteousness even as we live in this world (Deut. 20:19-20; 22:6-7; Ps. 24:1-2; Matt. 6:33; Luke 12:31; Eph. 1:9-10; Rev. 22:1-5).

*What is the
power of
Christ's
resurrection?*

6

PHILIPPIANS 3:1-4:1

Faith and Its Effects

In a Nutshell

God wants people who obey freely in every area of their lives, people who live for Christ without a sense of compulsion. As Paul writes to the Christians in Philippi, he insists that external Jewish customs do not accomplish this goal. The only way to be righteous, Paul insists, is through faith in the Lord Jesus, whose righteousness then becomes ours. This means that when we truly believe in Christ as Lord and Savior, we will want to do what God wants us to. We will be joined to Jesus in a new life, a resurrection life, and in this way we will know the power of Christ's resurrection.

Philippians 3

1Finally, my brothers, rejoice in the Lord! It is no trouble for me to write the same things to you again, and it is a safeguard for you.

2Watch out for those dogs, those men who do evil, those mutilators of the flesh. 3For it is we who are the circumcision, we who worship by the Spirit of God, who glory in Christ Jesus, and who put no confidence in the flesh— 4though I myself have reasons for such confidence.

If anyone else thinks he has reasons to put confidence in the flesh, I have more: 5circumcised on the eighth day, of the people of Israel, of the tribe of Benjamin, a Hebrew of Hebrews; in regard to the law, a Pharisee; 6as for zeal, persecuting the church; as for legalistic righteousness, faultless.

7But whatever was to my profit I now consider loss for the sake of Christ. 8What is more, I consider everything a loss compared to the surpassing greatness of knowing Christ Jesus my Lord, for whose sake I have lost all things. I consider them rubbish, that I may gain Christ 9and be found in him, not having a righteousness of my own that comes from the law, but that which is through faith in Christ—the righteousness that comes from God and is by faith. 10I want to know Christ and the power of his resurrection and the fellowship of sharing in his sufferings, becoming like him in his death, 11and so, somehow, to attain to the resurrection from the dead.

12Not that I have already obtained all this, or have already been made perfect, but I press on to take hold of that for which Christ Jesus took hold of me. 13Brothers, I do not consider myself yet to have taken hold of it. But one thing I do:

Forgetting what is behind and straining toward what is ahead, 14I press on toward the goal to win the prize for which God has called me heavenward in Christ Jesus. 15All of us who are mature should take such a view of things. And if on some point you think differently, that too God will make clear to you. 16Only let us live up to what we have already attained.

17Join with others in following my example, brothers, and take note of those who live according to the pattern we gave you. 18For, as I have often told you before and now say again even with tears, many live as enemies of the cross of Christ.

19Their destiny is destruction, their god is their stomach, and their glory is in their shame. Their mind is on earthly things. 20But our citizenship is in heaven. And we eagerly await a Savior from there, the Lord Jesus Christ, 21who, by the power that enables him to bring everything under his control, will transform our lowly bodies so that they will be like his glorious body.

Philippians 4:1

Therefore, my brothers, you whom I love and long for, my joy and crown, that is how you should stand firm in the Lord, dear friends!

A Digression

So far in his letter to the Philippians Paul has been writing about his situation in Rome and about what may or may not happen to him. He has also taken the time to encourage the Philippians in living for Jesus—understanding that they may often have to deal with suffering for Jesus' sake and that they are called to live humbly and faithfully after the pattern of Jesus himself.

At this point in the letter, though, we can detect a change in the flow of Paul's train of thought. Maybe he has stopped dictating the letter for a while. We can imagine, for example, that he may not have written it in one sitting, or even in one day. Whatever the case, it apparently occurs to Paul at this point that he should warn his friends about a serious problem that has developed among Christians of Jewish descent.

He starts by saying, "Finally . . . rejoice in the Lord!" (Phil. 3:1). And then another thought—about being wary of Jewish Christians who preach circumcision—enters in, and Paul goes on for a while in a sort of stream-of-consciousness style, as other important topics apparently occur to him. Then he finally picks up the thread of rejoicing again in Philippians 4:4.

This lesson, then, focuses on what Paul mentions during this digression in his letter. And he makes some very important points that tie in with earlier comments he has made about being sincere, faithful believers who know that their hope is only in Christ. Paul talks about true righteousness in Christ, knowing the power of Christ's resurrection and sharing in his sufferings, and pressing on toward the goal of glorious life forever in God's presence.

"Put No Confidence in the Flesh"
In Philippians 3:2 (and perhaps in the second half of 3:1) Paul takes up a theme that has recurred again and again in his ministry. It has to do with Christian Jews insisting that believers in Christ must still observe all the traditional Jewish rites—especially *circumcision.*

In an earlier letter Paul wrote to warn his friends in Galatia: "O foolish Galatians, who has bewitched you?" (Gal. 3:1). Some Jewish Christians had come to Galatia and had been persuading believers there that they had to observe circumcision and all other traditional Jewish rituals even though they had become converts to Christianity.

In his letter to the Philippians Paul is just as severe: "Watch out for those dogs, those men who do evil, those mutilators of the flesh" (Phil. 3:2). Paul clearly has not changed his mind on this subject!

He goes on to explain that what God desires is not people who "mutilate the flesh" but people "who worship by the Spirit of God, who glory in Christ Jesus, and who put no confidence in the flesh" (3:3). The physical, tangible, sensory rite of circumcision no longer has any validity—it is, after all, only a symbol. In Christ we now have the reality that circumcision pointed to—namely, being guided by the Holy Spirit. In other words, by the power of the Spirit we serve God not by our own flawed attempts at righteousness but by the righteousness of Christ, who fulfilled the law on our behalf. Paul knows that the more people depend on visual, tangible symbols, the less they depend on the Spirit of God. He knows it is wrong for Christians still to have "confidence in the flesh," as do the legalists of his day (3:3-4).

Two Kinds of Righteousness
Moving on to explain from his own experience, Paul says, "If anyone else thinks he has reasons to put confidence in the flesh, I have more" (3:4). Then he lists a number of his own qualifications, summing up that as far as righteousness by the law is concerned, he was "faultless" (3:6). Paul does this to show that he can evaluate the rituals of the law not as an outsider looking in, but as one who was once himself "a Pharisee," a strict observer of the literal details of law.

But there is something even more important than the law, Paul continues. All the righteousness of the law, as important as he used to think it was, becomes like "rubbish" when he sees that the righteousness necessary for salvation "comes from God and is by faith" (3:9).

There are two kinds of righteousness, and we need to think seriously about the difference. The first kind is a righteousness of rules. If your religion consists mainly of making sure you do some things and not do other things, then you have a legal system that is similar, at least in concept, to the law that was taught among Jews in Paul's day. From the teachings of the Old Testament (old covenant) it was clear that if a person could keep all the regulations of the law—that is, the law of Moses—that person would be righteous before God. The trouble, though, was that no sinner could keep the law perfectly. Paul himself notes this fact in his earlier letter to the Romans, where he says, quoting Psalms 14 and 53, "No one is righteous, not even one" (Rom. 3:10). A few lines later he explains,

> Now a righteousness from God, apart from law, has been made known, to which the Law and the Prophets testify. This righteousness from God comes through faith in Jesus Christ to all who believe. There is no difference, for all have sinned and fall short of the glory of God, and are justified freely by his grace through the redemption that came by Christ Jesus. (Rom. 3:21-24)

The only one ever to keep the law perfectly was Jesus Christ, the sinless Son of God. So Jesus is the only one who has been or ever will be declared righteous by the law.

Through the free gift of God, though, there is a second kind of righteousness. It comes by faith in Jesus, since he not only fulfilled the law but also died in our place to satisfy the law's requirements for our sake.

When we believe in Jesus as Lord and Savior, we understand that God does not judge us by our failures. God put our failures on Jesus' shoulders when he died on the cross for us. Jesus bore the punishment we deserved for sin so that we can enjoy the righteousness he earned. As a result, we are now freed to live by the Spirit of Jesus, who empowers us to live for God by keeping the law without being judged by the law.

Paul realized firsthand that he could never have "a righteousness of [his] own that comes from the law," so he gratefully accepted the free gift of "righteousness that comes from God and is by faith" in Christ (Phil. 3:9). He also passionately wanted his Christian friends in Philippi (and in Galatia and elsewhere) to enjoy this gift, so he tried his best to convince them to believe only in the righteousness that is by Christ alone.

The Power of Christ's Resurrection

Paul continues his discussion now in a way that may surprise us, saying, "I want to know Christ and the power of his resurrection" (3:10). What does he mean by this?

Paul appears to be using an analogy here similar to one he uses in Romans 6:1-14 to describe how we, as believers, die with Christ to our old life of sin and rise to new life in him. Paul seems to be talking about the same thing also in 2 Corinthians 5:17, where he writes, "If anyone is in Christ, he is a new creation; the old has gone, the new has come!" Knowing the power of Christ's resurrection—that is, the power (*dunamis*) of new life in Christ—means that we become like Christ and thus also share "in his sufferings" (Phil. 3:10) as we live for our Lord in this world.

In line with this we also become "like him in his death" (3:10). Paul uses similar language in Romans 8:36, where he quotes Psalm 44:22, saying, "For your sake we face death all day long; we are considered as sheep to be slaughtered." Another similar passage is 2 Corinthians 4:10, where Paul says, "We always carry around in our body the death of Jesus, so that the life of Jesus may also be revealed in our body." Since Paul may also be wondering about the outcome of his trial with Caesar, he may even be thinking here that he might *literally* become "like [Jesus] in his death," dying for the sake of God's kingdom and the spread of the gospel. And if that happens, Paul knows, he will surely one day "attain to the resurrection from the dead" (3:10-11), when all "the dead in Christ will rise" on the great day of the Lord's second coming (1 Thess. 4:16).

As Paul thinks about these things, he adds, "I press on toward the goal to win the prize for which God has called me heavenward in Christ Jesus" (Phil. 3:14). Just as runners in a race would press on toward the finish line to gain the winner's prize, Paul strains to keep living for Christ in the power of Christ, and he coaches the Philippians to do the same. "Let us live up to what we have already attained," he urges them. "Join with others in following my example . . . and take note of those who live according to the pattern we gave you" (3:16-17)— which, of course, is the pattern of the attitude of Christ (2:5).

Each of us must die to the ways of sin and rise again in the power of Christ's Spirit as we live the new life of faith. That's how we too know the power of Christ's resurrection. We are to "press on" as long as we live, always toward "the goal" of becoming the kind of person Jesus wants us to be.

Our Citizenship in Heaven

Paul also reminds the Philippians that in our new life in Christ we are already now citizens of heaven. "Our citizenship is in heaven" (3:20) because that's where Jesus is. When we share in his death and resurrection to new life, we also, in a sense, share in his ascension to heaven, where he rules at the right hand of God over all things (Eph. 1:20). In Ephesians 2:6 Paul goes so far as to say that God has "raised us up with Christ and seated us with him in the heavenly realms in Christ Jesus." Amazing!

As a result we may confidently expect that the Savior whom "we eagerly await . . . from there" will, "by the power that enables him to bring everything under his control" (Phil. 3:20-21), take us as we are and begin to transform us, already in this life, into his image (2 Cor. 3:18). And when he comes again, this awesome Savior will transform us fully so that "our lowly bodies . . . will be like his glorious body" (Phil. 3:21).

Standing Firm in the Lord

Philippians 4:1 summarizes what Paul has been saying in the preceding paragraphs: "Therefore . . . you whom I love and long for, my joy and crown, that is how you should stand firm in the Lord, dear friends!" How should the people stand firm? By being joined to Jesus in faith, as Paul has been describing.

More specifically this means dying with Jesus and rising with him. Believers are "in the Lord" already because they believe in Christ. Now they must make sure they stay there—working out their salvation as the Lord works in them (2:12-13). They must continue to live in such a way as to show the power of Christ's resurrection in their daily living (3:10). They must live in Christ each day, knowing that their "citizenship is in heaven" (3:20).

Additional Notes

3:3—"It is we who are the circumcision." In Paul's day it was customary to divide people into two groups, Jews and Gentiles. Since circumcision was a sign of the covenant between God and the Jewish people, the term *circumcision* came to be another name for the Jews as the people of God (see Gal. 2:12; Eph. 2:11). Now Paul is claiming that term for Christians as the new people of God in Christ. Paul means that literal circumcision is not important to God; what's important is that people live in covenant faithfulness to

God. The fact that the Jewish leaders had rejected Jesus and continued to oppose the gospel means, according to Paul, that they are breaking the covenant. So covenantal faithfulness is being practiced now by Christians, not by Jews. We Christians, Paul says, are the circumcision, the people who keep the covenant. We worship by the Spirit of God and "put no confidence in the flesh" (3:3).

3:15-16—"All of us who are mature should take such a view of things. And if on some point you think differently, that too God will make clear to you. Only let us live up to what we have already attained." Interesting! It's not clear what Paul specifically means when he says somebody might not agree with him on some point. But he does recognize that people have differing religious opinions. That does not seem to bother Paul. He's saying, in effect, *Let God take care of the little differences. In the meantime, as you run the race of faith, make sure you live up to what you already know.*

3:18—"Many live as enemies of the cross of Christ." Paul may be speaking of people who are still friends of the Christians in Philippi but who are not believers in Christ. Any of us who have non-Christian friends need to take note that ultimately these friends oppose our Lord, so we need to pray for their salvation and be sure that we ourselves are not dragged back into the mindsets and lifestyles of people who do not live for the Lord.

4:1—"Stand firm in the Lord." Paul does not mean here that we should never change our minds. Jesus told his disciples that the Holy Spirit would come and would guide them "into all truth" (John 16:13). When we become believers in Christ, the Spirit leads and guides us and always continues to do so in our lives. A Christian person who adamantly refuses ever to change his or her mind could well be resisting the Spirit, who may be trying to reveal something more of the truth about Jesus.

GENERAL DISCUSSION

1. Why might Christians of Jewish descent be so concerned about circumcising their sons? What does Paul mean by saying, "Watch out for those dogs" (Phil. 3:2)?

2. What does Paul mean when he says, "It is we who are the circumcision" (Phil. 3:3)?

3. Why does Paul spend so much time detailing his own legalistic righteousness? (See Phil. 3:4-6.)

4. Should we regard our rituals today as legalistic "rubbish"? (See Phil. 3:7-9.)

5. What does Paul mean by saying he wants to know the power of Christ's resurrection? (See Phil. 3:10-11.)

6. What is "the goal" Paul is speaking of in Philippians 3:14? Should we be pressing on toward this goal too? Or is this just for "spiritual giants" like Paul? Explain.

7. What does Paul mean when he writes that "our citizenship is in heaven" (Phil. 3:20)?

SMALL GROUP SESSION IDEAS

Opening (10-15 minutes)

Pray—Open with prayer, giving thanks for the opportunity to study God's Word together and to learn more about living the Christian life. Ask that you may be open to the Spirit's teaching and that you may be able to apply this lesson material to your everyday lives.

Share—Talk briefly with each other about goals, group projects, or items in the lesson material that you may have found unusual, surprising, or confusing.

Focus—Ask, *What does God want me to focus on in this lesson that will help me in my spiritual growth? What does our group (or church) most need to focus on?*

Growing (35-40 minutes)

Read—Perhaps the best way to read the Scripture for this lesson, since it covers several important topics, is to have as many people as possible take turns reading sentences or paragraphs. You may also wish to read or review portions of the study guide notes before moving into your discussion time.

Discuss—Along with the General Discussion questions you may want to include the following process questions wherever they fit best:

- If a leader like Paul were writing to your church, what sorts of traditions and customs do you think he'd say were important or unimportant for being a Christian in today's world? Why?

- Think of times when you've really strived to know God better or to grow more deeply spiritual. Was the effort worthwhile for you? Share your thoughts with the rest of the group. If the effort didn't seem to "pay off," try to think through what your motives or expectations were. Did they match up with things the apostle Paul has been teaching in his letter to the Philippians? Why or why not?

- If someone (let's say a neighbor or a child in Sunday school) asked you what it means to be a citizen of the kingdom of heaven, what would you say? (In your answer, try to give examples of things you do in your work, your recreational activities, and your worship that show how you give glory to God.)

Goalsetting (5 minutes)

Try the following goalsetting idea as a response to this lesson (or use an idea of your own):

- As a group, think together about pressing on toward the goal of full life in Christ—that is, as full as it can possibly be in this broken world. What kinds of things can you do together to build each other up and show others that you are alive in Christ?

Closing (10-15 minutes)

Preparing for Prayer—Share prayer requests and praises that you'd like to include at this time. You may also wish to mention goals and group projects you may be working on.

Prayer—Maybe you'd like to offer brief, one-sentence prayers this time, with everyone praying as he or she feels led. If so, simply open by having one of you begin, and then, when everyone's had a chance to offer a prayer or two (or more), someone can close. Thank God for hearing all your prayers, and ask for help each day as you "press on" to live for Jesus.

Optional Reading—At some point during your closing time, you may want to read aloud together Q&A 86 of the Heidelberg Catechism as an explanation of why we "press on" to live by the power of Christ's resurrection, as Paul urges us to:

**Q. We have been delivered
from our misery
by God's grace alone through Christ
and not because we have earned it:
why then must we still do good?**

A. To be sure, Christ has redeemed us by his blood.
But we do good because
Christ by his Spirit is also renewing us to be like himself,
so that in all our living
we may show that we are thankful to God
for all he has done for us,
and so that he may be praised through us.

And we do good
so that we may be assured of our faith by its fruits,
and so that by our godly living
our neighbors may be won over to Christ.

Dealing with
conflict by
moving toward
peace.

7

PHILIPPIANS 4:2-9

The Peace of God

In a Nutshell
There's no way we can completely avoid disagreement. But we can make a difference in the way we handle disagreements. Above all, we need to retain respect for people we disagree with, recognizing that, like Euodia and Syntyche in Philippi, we are all fellow servants of the Lord.

Instead of dwelling on disagreements, we need to be thinking about how we can be one in serving the Lord, attaining to the good and the beautiful, the noble and the admirable, to the glory of God. Then we can rejoice in experiencing "the peace of God" that passes beyond "all understanding" (Phil. 4:7).

Philippians 4:2-9
2I plead with Euodia and I plead with Syntyche to agree with each other in the Lord. 3Yes, and I ask you, loyal yokefellow, help these women who have contended at my side in the cause of the gospel, along with Clement and the rest of my fellow workers, whose names are in the book of life.

4Rejoice in the Lord always. I will say it again: Rejoice! 5Let your gentleness be evident to all. The Lord is near. 6Do not be anxious about anything, but in everything, by prayer and petition, with thanksgiving, present your requests to God. 7And the peace of God, which transcends all understanding, will guard your hearts and your minds in Christ Jesus.

8Finally, brothers, whatever is true, whatever is noble, whatever is right, whatever is pure, whatever is lovely, whatever is admirable—if anything is excellent or praiseworthy—think about such things. 9Whatever you have learned or received or heard from me, or seen in me—put it into practice. And the God of peace will be with you.

Euodia and Syntyche
As Paul nears the end of his letter to the Philippians, he knows he needs to mention a situation he's heard about, and he finds a way to tie it in with advice that helps his readers focus on peace in the Lord. The situation Paul needs to mention is a conflict that has developed between two women who have

previously "contended at [his] side in the cause of the gospel." He knows them well, and he mentions them by name: "Euodia and Syntyche" (Phil. 4:2).

Apparently Epaphroditus has told Paul about their disagreement. So now Paul pleads with them "to agree with each other in the Lord" (4:2). We have no indication what their disagreement was about, but apparently it was serious enough to cause trouble in the congregation.

Paul calls on another person in the church as well. This person is also an old friend, and Paul is counting on him to help: "I ask you, loyal yokefellow, help these women who have contended at my side in the cause of the gospel, along with Clement and the rest of my fellow workers, whose names are in the book of life." This friend (possibly named *Syzygus?*—the translation is uncertain) may well be one of the elders of the church, someone who probably had some standing and enough experience to try to get the quarreling pair to come to terms with each other, at least to make their opinions less divisive.

"In the Lord" is the crucial phrase here (4:2). If Euodia and Syntyche can agree with one another "in the Lord," they will serve as a fine example of believers who can put aside their differences for Jesus' sake.

Division is seldom, if ever, a good thing. And in comparison to churches in our society today, it would have been much more disastrous for the church in Philippi to be divided. But from this example of contention among church members we can learn that we can differ without losing respect for one another. We all follow the same Lord (see Eph. 4:1-6; Phil. 2:1-5). That truth must always be the unifying center of our faith, and it must shape our relationships with one another.

The Peace of God

Paul next indicates that the focus of the church should not be on differences but on the positive things we all share in Christ. Most of all, believers should "rejoice in the Lord" because of all Christ has done for us.

At last Paul picks up again the thread of discussion that he left hanging in 3:1 (in response to what he was saying in chap. 2; see 2:17-18). "Rejoice in the Lord always," he says. "I will say it again: Rejoice!" (4:4). In other words, just as Paul wants to focus on the good that can come out of his imprisonment and even his death, if that happens (2:17-18), the church will do well not to get bogged down in fighting and bickering but to focus on the goodness and blessing that believers have together in Christ.

Christians do have points of disagreement, but they must be careful not to let their arguments make them disagreeable, hard to live with, violent, emotional, critical. Paul counsels, "Let your gentleness be evident to all" (4:5). It's important that each believer be an obviously peaceable person, not given to conflict but gentle even to those with whom he or she disagrees.

Paul next states a rather curious reason for his advice: "The Lord is near" (4:5). What's the connection between the Lord's being near and our being gentle? Paul is not referring here to Christ's second coming—as if that should make a difference in the way we act one day compared to the way we act another day when we are already born again in Christ (John 3:5-8; 2 Cor. 5:17). Paul is simply reminding the believers in Philippi—and us—that the Lord Jesus is already now very close to us. Jesus is always near through the presence and power of the Holy Spirit.

Before he ascended to heaven, Jesus said to his disciples, "I am with you always, to the very end of the age" (Matt. 28:20). So Jesus is right here with us now, and we need to live accordingly. We ought not to let any unchristian spirit invade our conversation or our attitude toward others. In a sense, the Lord is looking over our shoulder, listening to everything we say, examining our thoughts and attitudes—always. In a way, Paul is admonishing, *Do you want to "work out your salvation" (Phil. 2:12)? Then do your best to be faithful images of the Lord Jesus. Don't be a quarreling, cantankerous, hard-to-get-along-with person.* "Let your gentleness be evident to all" (4:5).

In addition, Paul is saying, *Throw away your anxieties and, through the wonderful gift of prayer, lay them at the feet of God. Unload your concerns and troubles and, with thankfulness for all the Lord has done (and will continue to do) for you, let God take care of your troubles as only God can.* In this comforting advice (4:6) Paul is echoing the counsel of Jesus, who said, "Do not worry about your life. . . . But seek first [God's] kingdom and his righteousness, and all these things will be given to you as well" (Matt. 6:25, 33). "Come to me, all you who are weary and burdened, and I will give you rest. Take my yoke upon you and learn from me, for I am gentle and humble in heart, and you will find rest for your souls" (11:28-29). When we remember that "the Lord is near" and we can bring "everything" to God in prayer, says Paul, then "the peace of God, which transcends all understanding, will guard [our] hearts and [our] minds in Christ Jesus" (Phil. 4:7).

Neither you nor the person you are arguing with understands everything, so you don't have to get unreasonable or even anxious about someone disagreeing with you. You can remain at peace with him or her; you can agree to disagree. That yields a peace that goes beyond understanding, beyond rational agreement.

When our focus is on God and on how we can glorify God in all we do, despite disagreements and other troubles, the result is peace (*shalom*). Whenever we have disagreements or face troubles of any kind, the best thing we can do is focus on God.

Think About These Things

All this is good counsel, but we may find it hard to put into practice. Many of us get so excited and agitated by certain disagreements that we can't get them out of our heads. We can't get to sleep at night because we are worrying and rehashing problems over and over in our minds. So Paul urges an alternative: "Whatever is true, whatever is noble, whatever is right, whatever is pure, whatever is lovely, whatever is admirable—if anything is excellent or praiseworthy—think about such things" (4:8). We need to set our minds to thinking about better things. We need to get off the negative track and focus on the positive. Again, we need to focus on God and all the goodness and blessing God has given—"anything that is excellent and praiseworthy"—anything that helps us to focus again on glorifying God.

As we focus on God, we can remember to pray and to keep on praying (4:6). We can let God know how we feel. We can trust that God will always listen to us.

We may not get an immediate answer from God to end our troubles, but prayer will certainly remind us that God may well see things differently from the way we or our opponents do. Because prayer is communication with God, it will remind us that God knows what's happening even if we don't. God is in control. Prayer reminds us that we can leave the problem to God to settle. And that will, at least to some extent, help us to settle down and stop being disturbed by what's going on.

We can take Paul's advice here in general ways in our day-to-day living as well. For example, it's easy to become so obsessed with what's going wrong in our lives, in our churches, in our government, in television, in society, in our whole world, that we can develop a consistently negative, critical, accusatory outlook on things. But Paul urges us to think about "whatever is true . . . noble . . . right . . . pure . . . lovely . . . admirable . . .

excellent . . . praiseworthy" (4:8). Didn't Jesus say, "All authority in heaven and on earth has been given to me" (Matt. 28:18)? Doesn't the book of Revelation say, "The kingdom of the world has become the kingdom of our Lord and of his Christ" (Rev. 11:15)? Paul wants the Christians in Philippi— and all of us, for that matter—to be thinking about what Jesus is accomplishing now from heaven, not what Satan and the forces of evil are continuing to do. In Christ we need to focus on positive, healthy, admirable, wonderful things, not negative, destructive, damnable things.

And in case the people in the Philippian church wouldn't quite know how to do that, Paul says, in effect, *Imitate me. I live in Christ, and you can take that as an example of how to imitate Christ. And when you live that way, "the God of peace will be with you"* (Phil. 4:9). Paul is not speaking in a prideful way here. Instead he's coaching the Philippians to keep going in the Lord, to keep pressing on as he himself does, in the power of Christ's resurrection (3:10, 12).

God and Peace

Did you notice the two phrases in Philippians 4:7 and 4:9? Verse 7 speaks of "the peace of God," and verse 9 speaks of "the God of peace." We must strive to live with one another by focusing on the Lord, and "the peace of God . . . will guard" our hearts and minds "in Christ Jesus" (4:7). And as we strive to imitate Christ in a way like Paul has shown in his life, we can be assured that the "God of peace" will be with us.

Actually, as Jesus promised, he is with us "always" (Matt. 28:20), and as Paul points out earlier in this letter, our Lord is already working in us as we work out our salvation by striving to be like Christ (Phil. 2:12-13). But perhaps in our anxiety or trouble, even when we pray to God and strive to focus on God, we forget or we just can't see that God is "the God of peace" who is always with us. So Paul reminds us of that fact.

When we remember that "the Lord is near," we will be able to enjoy—even "rejoice" in—"the peace of God" (4:4-7). And when we "think about" all things good and wonderful and excellent and praiseworthy, remembering that these come from the God who is in control of all things, we'll be aware again, as we calm down, that "the God of peace" is with us, as always.

Additional Notes

4:4—"Rejoice in the Lord always." This is more than some emotional high that we're supposed to try to attain. No one can live on an emotional high all the time. It points to a consistent attitude toward life in general that comes from a strong faith that God is in control of all things, even bad things. No matter how bad circumstances may become— such as Paul being in prison unjustly for more than two years and still waiting for his trial—we must keep in mind that nothing is going to stop the Lord from going about his business of redeeming this world. With that frame of mind, we can rejoice always, even when things are going very badly for us. We can rejoice not that things are going badly, but that, despite these troubles, Christ is ruling at the right hand of God and is drawing people to himself (John 12:32; Eph. 1:20).

4:6—"In everything, by prayer and petition, with thanksgiving, present your requests to God." In this bit of advice we need to notice how important the phrase "with thanksgiving" is. We can be praying to God all the time, petitioning for this or that, and expecting God to answer just the way we want. And when it doesn't happen, we can become discouraged and disappointed. But we may be praying "with wrong motives," as James 4:3 suggests in the midst of another discussion on dealing with conflict and anxiety. If we have the attitude that God should go along with whatever we want, God may well filter out everything we say because our heart is not right. We have to try to see things from God's point of view. God is in control and is doing everything necessary to achieve what God is intending to achieve. If we indeed see that happening, we'll have an attitude of appreciation for all God is doing in this world—and that's the thanksgiving Paul is talking about. When we pray, we need to try our best to pray within God's will, as Jesus did (Luke 22:42).

4:7—"The peace of God . . . will guard your hearts and your minds in Christ Jesus." Recall that a bit earlier Paul has been talking about standing firm in the Lord (4:1). Here Paul is getting at the same thing. If you can become the kind of Christian who is gentle, rejoicing, prayerful, and thankful, then your mind will be guarded in peace from falling away from the Lord. Remain faithful in Christ and work out the

meaning of your salvation in your heart and life and mind,
as Christ works his will in you (4:12-13).

GENERAL DISCUSSION

1. Reflect on what Paul says about Euodia and Syntyche and
   handling their disagreement. What does this advice teach us
   about handling disagreements in the church?

2. In what sense is the Lord near (Phil. 4:5)?

3. How can you tell whether you have "the peace of God" that
   "transcends all understanding" (Phil. 4:7)?

4. Be honest with yourself—are you the kind of person Paul
   describes in Philippians 4:8, the kind who thinks about
   things that are true, noble, right, pure, lovely, admirable?
   What kind of mentality do you have—one that sees first
   what is good (what God does) or what is bad (what the
   forces of evil do)?

5. Would you dare to say, *Imitate me in the way I live,* as Paul
   does in Philippians 4:9? Why or why not?

SMALL GROUP SESSION IDEAS

Opening (10-15 minutes)

Pray—Open with prayer, thanking the Lord for bringing you
together again to study God's Word, asking for the Spirit's

guidance into truth, and praying for wisdom and patience when dealing with troubling situations.

Share—Use this time to share briefly how things are going with goals or projects you may be working on. You might also like to look back and mention some of the things you've learned about Philippians and about Christian living so far in this Bible study.

Focus—While working through the lesson material, try to focus on the following questions: *In what ways does conflict in the church affect me? What can I, as a part of my church (or group), do "in the Lord" when conflict arises?*

Growing (35-40 minutes)

Read—One way to read the Scripture for this lesson would be to have three readers and three summarizers—a reader for each of the paragraphs (Phil. 4:2-3, 4-7, 8-9) and a person to summarize the main point of each paragraph after it's read. You may also want to read or review parts of the study guide notes before moving on to the discussion questions.

Discuss—Because of the subject matter for this session several of the General Discussion questions call for in-depth personal reflection. It's important, of course, for everyone to be sensitive to one another while discussing personal matters. And yet it's profitable for us as believers in Christ to dig into our own experiences and to confront openly and honestly what we may have done in ignorance or selfishness. We all need to submit to the transforming work of the Spirit in our lives, and to do that we need to face up to our own shortcomings. If someone in the group does lay open some old wounds, be sure to respond with understanding and support.

Along with the General Discussion questions you may wish to touch on some of the following process questions:

- Reflect on examples of conflict or trouble in your church that have been (or are being) resolved. In what ways have these situations been handled "in the Lord" (Phil. 4:2)?

- Spend a few minutes reflecting on things that are "excellent and praiseworthy" (4:8) in your group, your church, your community, your nation, and this world. Share your thoughts with each other, describing ways in which these things glorify God.

- Do you know (of) anyone who points others to Christ through an excellent example of servanthood and dependence on God, as Paul did? (See 1 Timothy 1:12-17.) If so, in what ways has this person's example helped to encourage you in living by faith? In giving glory to God?

Goalsetting (5 minutes)
In response to the material for this lesson, try the following goalsetting idea for at least a week (and you may wish to keep it up indefinitely!):

- Identify (privately) a trait mentioned in today's lesson that you feel is somewhat lacking in your life, and set a goal of praying every day specifically for growth in that area. Ask the Spirit to be near you and to guide you to grow in the way God wants you to. Also invite the Spirit to show you other areas in your life in which you need to grow to be more like Christ.

Closing (10-15 minutes)
Preparing for Prayer—As you mention items you'd like others to pray about, include situations or issues that may have come up during your discussion time. For example, would you like to ask for God's help in getting along better with someone else (unnamed)? Or to rid yourself of a spirit of jealousy toward someone? Or to love someone who is difficult even to be with? Also mention goals or group projects you'd like prayer for.

Prayer—After everyone has had an opportunity to offer prayers for each other, you may wish to close by saying the Lord's Prayer together, perhaps with everyone holding hands as a symbol of your oneness in Christ.

Optional Singing—You could also close with a song that fits the lesson material, such as "Rejoice, O Pure in Heart" or "To God Be the Glory."

Group Study Project (Optional)
If any of you would like to learn more about prayer, you may wish to study it sometime as a group or as individuals. Here's a brief list of resources on prayer to get you started:

- *Teaching P.R.A.Y.E.R.: Guidance for Pastors and Church Leaders* (Abingdon, 2001) by Brant D. Baker
- *Too Busy Not to Pray,* second ed. (InterVarsity, 1998), by Bill Hybels
- *Intercession* (Servant Publications, 2001) by Dutch Sheets

- *The Praying Church Sourcebook,* second ed. (CRC Publications, 1997), by Alvin J. Vander Griend
- *The Praying Church Idea Book* (CRC Publications, 2001) by Douglas A. Kamstra
- *Developing a Prayer-Care-Share Lifestyle* (HOPE Ministries, 1999), devotions written by Alvin J. Vander Griend, Edith Bajema, John F. DeVries, and David J. Deters

You can learn more about these and other titles online at www.FaithAliveResources.org, or call 1-800-333-8300 for assistance or for a free printed catalog.

*What's "the
secret of being
content"?*

8

PHILIPPIANS 4:10-23

Generosity and Contentment

In a Nutshell

Paul weaves two themes together in the closing section of his letter: the Philippians' generosity and his own contentment. Paul expresses his gratitude to the Philippians for their thoughtfulness in sending him financial support, and he assures them that all his needs are being met and that he's satisfied. "I have learned the secret of being content in any and every situation," he writes (Phil. 4:12).

As always, the apostle also turns the center of attention away from himself and his readers to Christ. "I can do everything through him who gives me strength," says Paul, and "God will [also] meet all your needs according to his glorious riches in Christ Jesus" (4:13, 19). These are lessons we all need to learn.

Philippians 4:10-23

10I rejoice greatly in the Lord that at last you have renewed your concern for me. Indeed, you have been concerned, but you had no opportunity to show it. 11I am not saying this because I am in need, for I have learned to be content whatever the circumstances. 12I know what it is to be in need, and I know what it is to have plenty. I have learned the secret of being content in any and every situation, whether well fed or hungry, whether living in plenty or in want. 13I can do everything through him who gives me strength.

14Yet it was good of you to share in my troubles. 15Moreover, as you Philippians know, in the early days of your acquaintance with the gospel, when I set out from Macedonia, not one church shared with me in the matter of giving and receiving, except you only; 16for even when I was in Thessalonica, you sent me aid again and again when I was in need. 17Not that I am looking for a gift, but I am looking for what may be credited to your account. 18I have received full payment and even more; I am amply supplied, now that I have received from Epaphroditus the gifts you sent. They are a fragrant offering, an acceptable sacrifice, pleasing to God. 19And my God will meet all your needs according to his glorious riches in Christ Jesus.

20To our God and Father be glory for ever and ever. Amen.

21Greet all the saints in Christ Jesus. The brothers who are with me send greetings. ²²All the saints send you greetings, especially those who belong to Caesar's household.

²³The grace of the Lord Jesus Christ be with your spirit. Amen.

Philippian Generosity
It may be that Paul stopped dictating his letter for a while before writing this closing section. Maybe he had unexpected visitors.

At any rate, in closing, he repeats some things he has said earlier. "I rejoice greatly in the Lord that at last you have renewed your concern for me. Indeed, you have been concerned, but you had no opportunity to show it" (Phil. 4:10; see 2:30). And a little later he goes on to say, "It was good of you to share in my troubles," and "I am amply supplied, now that I have received from Epaphroditus the gifts you sent" (4:14, 18; see 2:25).

Paul is especially indebted to this church in Philippi. He recalls that they are the only people who have consistently helped him financially through the years. "Not one church shared with me in the matter of giving and receiving, except you only; for even when I was in Thessalonica, you sent me aid again and again when I was in need" (4:15-16). And since that earlier time, Paul acknowledges, the Philippians certainly have been interested in what he's been doing, but it seems they've had no way to get support to him. "Indeed, you have been concerned," he says, "but you had no opportunity to show it" (4:10). Now, though, having heard he was in prison in Rome, they have again responded freely and generously (4:18).

The Secret of Contentment
In this passage Paul says some very profound things about his own attitude toward suffering. "I have learned to be content whatever the circumstances" (4:11). Notice that he says it is something he has "learned." He adds, "I know what it is to be in need, and I know what it is to have plenty" (4:12). He could be poor or rich; he could be living in prison or in a mansion. But he has learned how not to complain about deprivation and how not to waste resources when he has more than he needs.

There's a "secret" to learning contentment, says Paul. "I have learned the secret of being content in any and every situation, whether well fed or hungry, whether living in plenty or in want" (4:12).

And what's the secret Paul has learned? The answer is simple enough: "I can do everything through him who gives me strength" (4:13). Paul can handle any situation he is in because he looks to Jesus to provide the strength to respond to it. Of course, he doesn't mean he can decide to do something impossible, like swimming to the bottom of the Mediterranean Sea, and to call on Christ to give him the strength and ability to do it. Paul means that because he follows Christ's call to do everything for the sake of the gospel and for the glory of God (see 1 Cor. 10:31), the Lord will sustain him and enable him to manage whatever happens in the process.

The same is true for us. If you live your entire life in the faithful service of Jesus, he will provide you the strength to deal with any situation that comes up. It may not be easy, but if you constantly turn to the Lord, he will provide a way for you to handle any situation. You can learn to be content even if everything seems to go sour in your life. You "can do everything through him who gives [you] strength" (Phil. 4:13).

A Fragrant Offering

So Paul reiterates his thanks: "It was good of you to share in my troubles. . . . I have received full payment and even more; I am amply supplied, now that I have received from Epaphroditus the gifts you sent" (4:14, 18). At the same time, Paul wants to avoid the impression that he's always soliciting money for himself (as some evangelists today seem to do). Paul says he is more interested in the Philippians' spiritual welfare, as demonstrated in their thoughtfulness, than in the gifts they have sent: "Not that I am looking for a gift, but I am looking for what may be credited to your account" (4:17).

Paul, of course, is not implying works-righteousness here. He doesn't mean the Philippians have to do good works in order to get credit in their account before God. He means only that they have done the right thing in the sight of God by coming to Paul's assistance. Their gifts "are a fragrant offering, an acceptable sacrifice, pleasing to God" (4:18). In return for their generosity, which flows from them out of gratitude to Christ, Paul promises, "My God will meet all your needs according to his glorious riches in Christ Jesus" (4:19).

Does God really meet all our needs? Let's say your doctor diagnoses you as having cancer. Can you count on God to heal you of this disease so that you will not die from it? Or let's say you lose your job. Can you expect God to provide you with another one? Or maybe you have some obsessive sin that no one else knows about, or perhaps it's something people do know about—such as alcoholism or a drug addiction. Can you really believe God will enable you to conquer it? Or maybe you've simply done something really stupid, and you despise yourself for it. Will God really restore your self-respect—as well as the respect of others?

As we think about questions like these, it's important to distinguish between *need* and *want*. For example, of course you want to survive cancer, but do you need to? Or, of course you want to get another job, but is that what you need most at this time?

Paul is pointing out that in our Christian living we always need to be aware that God is in control of whatever circumstances take place in our lives. This does not mean we aren't responsible for actions that may have produced the situation we're in. It means that even though we may be directly responsible, God is giving us the opportunity to learn from our mistakes, to repent if needed, and to find new grace to live in obedience for Jesus' sake. God will provide whatever is necessary for us—whether it pleases us or not, whether it fills our wants or not. As creatures of the God who loves us and knows what's best for us, we need to accept whatever situation God places us in and to learn to be content with it.

Maybe you are aware of some fault in your spiritual life. Pray that God will help you overcome it. And know that if you do, you might receive an answer that's difficult for you to take. At some point, though, you'll be able to see that God's way is best, and you'll be grateful for it—as difficult as the situation may be. Paul, for example, prayed and prayed that God would remove his "thorn in [the] flesh," but God insisted that he had to learn to live with it (2 Cor. 12:7-8).

Final Greetings
Paul wants all glory to go "to our God and Father . . . for ever and ever" (Phil. 4:20). As he says goodbye, the apostle in prison sends greetings again to "all the saints in Christ Jesus" in Philippi (4:21; see 1:1), and he conveys greetings from all the Christians who are with him in Rome (4:21-22).

It's interesting that Paul mentions "especially those who belong to Caesar's household" (4:22). It would not be too many more years before Emperor Nero would begin a great persecution of Christians in Rome, not to mention in his own household. But for now, it appears, there are several Christians who are serving, perhaps as slaves and even as guards (1:13), in the royal establishment of Caesar's palace.

Paul ends his letter with a benediction similar to the one he opened with (1:1), and it may be that he inscribes these words with his own hand: "The grace of the Lord Jesus Christ be with your spirit. Amen" (4:23; see 2 Thess. 3:17). In this way Paul again encourages us to think again of Christ being with us (see 4:5, 9). We might get disheartened by troubles in our personal lives, in our families, in our church, in our nation, in this world—whatever. But if the Lord Jesus is "with [our] spirit" (4:23), we cannot be overcome by the negatives of life, by the forces of evil that would like to frighten us from serving God, "whatever the circumstances" (4:11). We can be assured that God knows how to wrest victory out of seeming defeat (see Col. 2:15). And we can rise with Jesus out of death into life—already now in this life (Phil. 3:10-11)!

Additional Notes

4:10—"no opportunity to show it." Paul knows the Christians in Philippi have been interested in assisting him in the spread of the gospel. But he knows also that they could not have known where he was at times, or whether he was in special need of assistance from time to time. So he does not want them to feel guilty for not having assisted him earlier.

4:12—"the secret of being content." Paul is not talking about being content to let things remain as they are, making no attempt to improve. What he means is that, in the process of working hard at whatever God gives us to do, we do not complain of difficulties that we must endure. We must work hard at serving the Lord in all we do every day, and if that involves suffering, we must learn to accept it without complaint against God. Of course, we may make improvements and changes to alleviate struggle—such as through invention and the use of technology—but these must also be within willing acceptance of the circumstances God puts us in.

4:12—"I have learned . . ." Contentment is something to be learned. It does not come naturally. How do we learn contentment? By experience—though not by experience all by itself. It has to be experience infused with faith. If we really believe God is in control of all things, we know God is in control of all the discouraging and damaging things that happen in life. So we live by faith, knowing that God is teaching us something even through bad things that happen, and in Christ's strength we can be content to struggle on (4:13).

4:16—"Even when I was in Thessalonica, you sent me aid again and again when I was in need." On Paul's second missionary journey, when he was forced out of town in Philippi, the next town he came to was Thessalonica. He encountered trouble in that city also (see Acts 17:1-9). Though we can't be sure, it seems that in Philippians 4:16 Paul may be referring to that situation. It's also possible that the people in Philippi kept sending assistance as Paul moved from town to town during that trip—to Berea, Athens, and even Corinth.

GENERAL DISCUSSION

1. Think back to earlier lessons that mentioned the main reason Paul wrote this letter to the Christians in Philippi. Using some of the passages in Philippians, how would you explain to someone else why Paul wrote this letter?

2. Think back on your life as a Christian, and reflect on a past sorrow that was extremely difficult for you. How did you handle it? Did it help you learn "the secret of being content" (4:11)?

3. Many of us don't spend much time thinking of difficult things that may yet happen to us, but in some ways it can be healthy to think of situations we might face in life—especially if it helps us prepare helpful, God-glorifying responses that we might not give otherwise. See if you can picture yourself in a challenging situation or two that you haven't yet encountered. Then look back to see if anything you've experienced before might help you somehow in these situations. Do you think you could handle these in a way like Paul does when he says, "I can do everything through him who gives me strength" (Phil. 4:13)? Explain.

4. A church member once said, "All the church is interested in is my money." Respond to this in the light of what Paul writes in Philippians 4:17: "Not that I am looking for a gift, but I am looking for what may be credited to your account."

5. In your experience, is it true that God meets all your needs (Phil. 4:19)? Can you tell of a time when God answered a prayer request in a way that made things more complicated or difficult for you? Explain.

SMALL GROUP SESSION IDEAS

Opening (10-15 minutes)
Pray—Open with a prayer that mentions the important matter of contentment we'll be discussing in this session. For example, you could pray, *Lord, help us all to learn the secret of contentment, as Paul did, through the many trials and challenges of daily life.* Ask also that God's Spirit may guide you in your discussion so that everyone may grow in faith, understanding, and obedience.

Share—Take time to report on goals or projects you've committed to. Or perhaps raise questions about things Paul says in the Scripture for this lesson or elsewhere in Philippians.

Focus—Throughout this session, challenge yourself to focus by asking, *Am I content? What difference can (or does) contentment make in my life? In my service for Christ and his church?*

Growing (35-40 minutes)
Read—Again you may wish to divide the reading into sections, with three readers and three summarizers, who can state the main point of each section after it's read. Readers could take the following sections: Philippians 4:10-13, 14-20, 21-23. You may also wish to read or review sections of the study guide notes.

Discuss—As you work through the General Discussion questions, you may also wish to include one or two additional process questions, if you have time.

- Highlight one or two things you've learned in this study of Philippians that you'd like to share with someone else. How would you explain it to a younger Christian who's never read Philippians before? How would you explain it to someone who may not be a Christian?

- Share some stories you've heard of other Christians who have put Paul's words about contentment into practice. In what ways do these stories inspire you? Frighten you? Give you peace? Explain.

Goalsetting (5 minutes)

One useful goal would be for each of you to pray at least once a day in the coming week for contentment about a disturbing condition in your life. (As you take on a goal like this, understand that you cannot pray for something continually without really wanting it to happen. If your prayer is on the unbelieving side, it probably won't be answered the way you want it to be. If you're in doubt about prayer, see John 15:1-8 and James 4:2-3, and ask the Spirit to help you pray in line with God's will for you.)

Closing (10-15 minutes)

Preparing for Prayer—Along with concerns and praises, mention items that may have come up during your discussion. Also include requests related to goals or projects you may be working on.

Prayer—Everyone should feel free to offer a short prayer during this closing prayer time. Of course, you may also pray silently about some things, and you could include a time of silence—say, thirty seconds or so—before closing with thanks and praise to God. In line with Paul's closing remarks in his letter to the Philippians, give God the glory for all you've learned from Philippians and about each other, and ask that "the grace of the Lord Jesus Christ be with your spirit" (Phil. 4:23).

Optional Singing—You may also wish to close with a song that fits with the theme of contentment, such as "When We Walk with the Lord" or "God Moves in a Mysterious Way."

Evaluation

Background

Size of group:
- [ ] fewer than 5 persons
- [ ] 5-10
- [ ] 10-15
- [ ] more than 15

Age of participants:
- [ ] 20-30
- [ ] 31-45
- [ ] 46-60
- [ ] 61-75 or above

Length of group sessions:
- [ ] under 60 minutes
- [ ] 60-75 minutes
- [ ] 75-90 minutes
- [ ] 90-120 minutes or more

Please check items that describe you:
- [ ] male
- [ ] female
- [ ] ordained or professional church staff person
- [ ] elder or deacon
- [ ] professional teacher
- [ ] church school or cate-chism teacher (three or more years' experience)
- [ ] trained small group leader

Study Guide and Group Process

Please check items that describe the material in the study guide:
- [ ] varied
- [ ] monotonous
- [ ] creative
- [ ] dull
- [ ] clear
- [ ] unclear
- [ ] interesting to participants
- [ ] uninteresting to participants
- [ ] too much
- [ ] too little
- [ ] helpful, stimulating
- [ ] not helpful or stimulating
- [ ] overly complex, long
- [ ] appropriate level of difficulty

Please check items that describe the group sessions:
- [ ] lively
- [ ] dull
- [ ] dominated by leader
- [ ] involved most participants
- [ ] relevant to lives of participants
- [ ] irrelevant to lives of participants
- [ ] worthwhile
- [ ] not worthwhile

In general I would rate this material as
☐ excellent
☐ very good
☐ good
☐ fair
☐ poor

Additional comments on any aspect of this Bible study:

Name (optional): _____
Church: _____
_____
City/State/Province: _____
_____

Please send completed form to

Word Alive / Philippians
Faith Alive Christian Resources
2850 Kalamazoo Ave. SE
Grand Rapids, MI 49560

Thank you!